PRESTO!

MAGIC FOR THE BEGINNER

Other books by the same author:

Days, Dates and Data
Amedeo's Continental Magic
Magic With Everyday Objects
Magic With Cards (Frank Garcia, co-author)

PRESTO!

MAGIC FOR THE BEGINNER

George Schindler

Illustrated by Ed Tricomi

BARNES
&NOBLE
BOOKS
NEW YORK

For Mom and Dad,
who thought it was only "naarishkeit."

CONTENTS

PREFACE

So you want to be a magician? Well, you've come to the right place, step into my office. This book was written for you, a person interested in learning the basics of this fascinating art. It is intended to outline the many kinds of tricks you can accomplish and how to accomplish them. It includes all the fun aspects of learning to entertain others. You will not need any special skills, expensive props, or long hours of practice. You will be able to perform most of the tricks immediately so that you can quickly realize the gratification of performing.

You can learn magic at any time of your life. My experience with the School for Magicians in New York has shown me that grandmothers learn as quickly as elementary school students. Magic is universally appealing to people in every walk of life. The students of magic have diversified backgrounds both in their education and professions. But magic hobbyists all have a single common denominator, that of learning to improve themselves and enriching their lives by entertaining others. Magic is the perfect vehicle with which to do this.

Once you have joined the magic fraternity, you will be meeting an unusual group of men and women, professional and amateur, filled with genuine camaraderie. No other group can equal their friendship. Perfect strangers become lifelong friends through magic, an art that has no boundaries. It is an art that offers you compeers in every part of the world.

Some of the sleight-of-hand techniques you are about to learn will need practice time. Most of the other things in the book do not. You should be able to make most of the props by yourself using common, everyday household objects. Start at the beginning and follow the chapters one at a time in sequence. My teaching technique is the same as I have used in my previous books. You must read the effects with props in hand. By the time you have finished reading and doing, you will see that you have performed the trick.

You will note that there are short quotations used after some of the chapter headings. These were taken from Book 13 of *The Discoverie of Witchcraft* written by Reginald Scot in 1584. It will serve as a reminder that our art is an ancient one. It should also humble the student to know that we are doing things the same way now as they did then.

This preface would not be complete without a few words of thanks to the many people instrumental in making my writing efforts worthwhile. Special thanks are in order to my partners at The School for Magicians. These are talented people like Arnold Freed, Fred Ponger, Frank Garcia, and our favorite instructor, Bob Elliott. I must also acknowledge some of the great students whose lives have changed with their newfound magical talents, and people like Bob Reiss, whose devotion to magic set him on a course bringing magic acts, books, and kits to thousands of young magicians. He has promoted the art and the appreciation of magic as has no one else in recent times.

And thanks to some of my other favorite students: Judy Lindenberg, the happy grandma, who is now a member of the board of directors of the Society of American Magicians in New York; Howie Bern, general manager of Grossinger's Hotel, whose personal warmth and charm qualify him to belong to our fraternity, even without his rope tricks; and Shelly Carol, who giggled her way through three magic courses to become a professional magician. And there are so many others—their names would fill a directory. They know who they are: Marvelous Marvin the Magnificent Magician, Mort, Barry, Joe, Andrew, Deborah, Steve, Eddie, take a bow.

Now let's get to work. We have a lot to do.

INTRODUCTION TO MAGIC

What strange things are brought to passe by naturall magicke.

Reginald Scot, DISCOVERIE OF WITCHCRAFT, 1584
Book XIII, Chapter IV

SOME HISTORY

In an age when rockets can go to the moon, pictures can pass through the air onto your TV screen, and chicken soup comes out of a plastic envelope, people believe that anything is possible. Nothing that looks mechanical will be accepted as anything other than modern scientific achievement. It wasn't always this way.

Magic is being able to create the impossible, defying the natural laws of science as we know them to be. It is being able to produce unusual effects and have the power to control events outside of our normal experiences. For thousands of years, before explanations were possible, people believed that the magician himself was a super being. Magic was the forerunner of religion. The search for answers to unexplained happenings prompted man to invent religion.

Today's magic is for the sole purpose of entertaining people. With new ways and means, we accomplish small miracles that seem impossible. But where did all this originate?

The secrets of the tricks performed by tribal magicians, dating almost back to prehistoric times, were passed from father to son. The high priest was a magician whose job it was to protect his people. He brought harm to their enemies. He conducted magical rituals for their benefit.

Archaeologist Henry Westcar unearthed a scroll in Egypt in

1823 that tells of magic performed about 4,000 years ago by Dedi the conjuror at the Royal Court of Khufu, the pharaoh of Egypt. Khufu was the builder of the famed Great Pyramid of Gizeh. The papyrus related the story of Dedi, 110 years old. The great magician cut off the head of a goose. He muttered a small chant and then set the bird on the ground, pressing the head to the body. The bird was restored to life and waddled away in perfect condition.

The hieroglyphics found on the walls of the Beni Hasan Temple depict magic dating back to 2500 B. C. The Old Testament tells of Aaron, who changed his rod into a serpent in the presence of the pharaoh. Around 600 B. C. the writer Zoroaster created the Persian Ahriman concept, tying magic and religion to Satan.

The Greeks later found astrology as the answer to the unknown laws of the universe. The beginnings of mathematics and medicine started scientific investigation, which overshadowed belief in magic. Magicians and students of black magic were wrapped in a veil of mystery and were often held in disrepute.

As Christianity spread, the practice of magic was tied to Satanism and black magic. Pope Alexander IV condemned all forms of magic in 1258. Anyone performing it after that time was considered a student of witchcraft. The classic conjuring trick was performed for entertainment, but the fear of black magic was so powerful that magic as we know it was condemned. The magician, depicted as a worker of the devil, was scorned.

In 1350 Marco Polo had seen magic in China. Magic had been reported around the world. The Hindus were performing their version of the Cups and Balls, the Chinese were doing the Linking Rings, and American Indians caused arrows to levitate inside their baskets.

Later, during the Middle Ages, street conjurors were still playing for the masses, as were court conjurors for royalty. The tricks of the early fourteenth century dealt with sleight of hand, coin and card tricks, cutting and restoring a rope, and torture tricks where bodies were severed and restored again. But the art was still not respectable.

In 1584 Reginald Scot, an English justice of the peace, wrote an exposé of magic, divorcing the conjuror from black magic. He accurately described sleight-of-hand methods and other tricks. It was the first book of its kind in the history of magic.

Charlatans were still fleecing their audiences with magic, stealing chickens and often slipping out of town without paying their bills. They were in the same category as jugglers and traveling gypsies. Respected for their entertaining skills, they still were not trusted. The street conjuror traveled with his bag of tricks, which was an apronlike affair with large pockets in which to store his various props. The apron was the symbol of the magician of that period. Many famous pieces of art depict the magician in his apron working with cups and balls.

In the early eighteenth century Isaac Fawkes hired a theater in London. Other magicians of that time were performing for the upper classes of society at private functions, but he was the first magician to charge admission. Along with other magicians who did the same, Fawkes elevated magic to a theater art. Gustavus Katterfelto of Prussia and Philip Breslaw of Germany were other magicians who followed suit.

Magic began to flourish in the East and in the West. Hindu and Indian magicians in Calcutta performed feats of mystery such as levitations and the famed Indian Rope Trick. Fakirs performed torture effects such as walking on hot coals or lifting heavy weights with their eyelids.

Modern stage magic became very popular in the early 1700s. People like Pinetti, Balsamo (the Great Cagliastro), Pilferer, and Decremps laid the groundwork for the magicians who followed. The performers who followed were even greater. They were men like Robert-Houdin, Hermann, Maskelyne, Kellar, Thurston, and Houdini.

In our own century, vaudeville gave us other fine magical names such as T. Nelson Downs, Malini, Frakson, Amedeo, Jarrow, Dante, Flosso, Keating, Ducrot, Dorny, Dunninger, and Blackstone. You will certainly be following the histories of these men as you learn more about our art.

You will watch modern magic with a new eye. You will see effects that were performed centuries ago, still the most popular of tricks. But today the techniques are geared to entertain people with a different presentation. Yes, we still fool them . . . but first we'll entertain them.

THREE CATEGORIES

The new student of magic will probably start with small magic and eventually work his way up to bigger things. The places that you play will determine the kind of magic you can perform. You wouldn't do a coin vanish in a large civic auditorium, nor would you saw a lady in half for an audience in your living room. There are three categories to consider.

Closeup Magic

This is not only the oldest form of the entertaining art but still one of the most popular. It has recently proven to be one of the most lucrative forms of the art. The increased use of magicians at cocktail parties, trade shows, and hospitality suites proves that this form is very much alive. Closeup magic requires skill in performing for small groups of people, literally under their noses. They may be sitting or standing right next to you, so you will need more deceptive talent rather than gimmicked bags and boxes. You will use everyday props that are easily carried in your pockets such as cards, coins, safety pins, string, matches, cigarettes, etc.

Presenting closeup magic requires the same standard principles of showmanship and suspense required for larger magic. It is more demanding and at the same time much more gratifying. Your audience can be as small as a single person. You can perform extemporaneously using the same psychology and misdirection as the stage performer. You will probably involve your spectators more directly, thus entertaining them better.

Club or Cabaret Magic

This is a broad term that includes magic for larger groups, taking in everything from living room audiences to those in school auditoriums, nightclubs, banquets, picnics, and so on. The audiences are larger and cannot see tiny pocket props. Since the props are larger, the magic must be bigger in scope and effect. Your props will now be carried in a suitcase, and you will need a small table to hold silk scarves, fishbowls, production boxes and tubes, flowers, canes, hats, candles, birds, etc.

You can use Egg Bags, Linking Rings, and Doves. Along with these larger props come other methods of using them. The hiding-places must be bigger than the palm of your hand. Your presentation must include staging, lighting, sound, clear patter, and stage presence. Club magic is the most popular form of the art practiced today.

Grand Illusion

The mechanical age brought larger illusions to the theaters of the world. Automatons and mechanical figures led the way to larger box illusions. These require transportation, assistants, stage crews, carpenters, and grand costumes. They are the spectaculars in magic. The Sawing a Lady in Half, Levitation, Metamorphosis, Zig Zag, Mis-Made Lady, and other large illusions can be seen only in the theater or on TV, where large stages can accommodate the equipment. They must also be accompanied by magicians who can move around the stage like actors or dancers with grace, poise, and drama. The assistants are well-rehearsed, and the illusions are breathtaking.

It should be obvious to the new magician that this book will deal with only the first two categories of performance. Aside from the experience needed for grand illusions, the expense is overwhelming.

I have included enough magic in Closeup and Club categories to provide you with the basis of an act in either area. The last chapter on showmanship and the presentation of magic will cover the aspects needed for all three categories.

MISDIRECTION – KEY TO MAGIC

Most people believe that the "hand is quicker than the eye." What they never realize is that their eyes are looking in the wrong place. The magician creates that condition with the use of misdirection.

In very simple terms misdirection is the art of diverting the spectator's eye as well as his mind. Its aim is to take attention away from what is actually happening. The spectator is led to believe a false premise. He sees only what the magician wants him to see.

Misdirection, as an art form, should be studied by the serious student of magic. The tricks in this book have built-in misdirection. A working knowledge of how this is accomplished will help you with other tricks and with all forms of magic.

A great trick is only as great as the performer. A good performer uses his skills to accomplish the impossible in the mind of the spectator. For it is the mind that interprets what the eye has seen. The techniques of this diversion vary with the kinds of effects that you will be performing. But the theory is always the same. The magician allows the spectator to make his own decision as to what he sees and thinks is true. But that decision is fully controlled by the magician. He allows the spectator to believe the false premise by misdirection. The first thing to learn about deception is that it depends upon the performer to show the spectator that he is not attempting to deceive him. Any con man will tell you this. If you don't want something to be seen, don't look at it yourself. Don't touch it, don't move toward it, don't let anyone else touch it. Act naturally and stay cool. To make sure that the spectators do not look in the wrong place, you must help them. The spectators' eyes will always follow yours. If you look at your left hand, they will look at your left hand. When you look directly at other people, they will look directly at you. Once the eye is taken away from the critical move, half the work is done.

When causing an object to vanish, you never look to where the object has been hidden. Instead your eyes travel to the place the object was supposed to be. The spectators' eyes will always follow a moving object. For instance, if you want to direct the attention away from the right hand, you move the left hand.

Every movement made by the magician should be natural. If there are times when your hands are not in a natural position, you will create that condition in advance a few times so that when you finally need the action, it goes unnoticed. This is called conditioning. If you are able to anticipate your spectators' natural suspicions, you can direct their attention elsewhere at the right time.

Having your spectators take part in a physical action as part of your trick can also divert attention. If you have an object in the opposite hand and want a little more attention, you can ask a spectator to *"blow"* or to *"pass your hand over the coin."*

In many of the tricks using props you will find that the apparatus often looks like something it isn't. The disguise of props is another way in which the audience is deceived. A fake egg looks like a real one, a load chamber is disguised as a glass of milk, and so on.

Your patter is a very strong tool used in the art of misdirection. To make your patter sound believable you must believe what you say. The little white lie helps to tell it like it isn't. If you say that the *"little ball goes into the hat,"* why shouldn't they believe you? After all, you're a nice person. Be cautious not to be caught in a lie. And above all, patter must never give unnecessary attention to information the audience does not have to know. *"A fresh egg,"* can describe the fake egg rather than *"a real egg."* No need to give anyone the idea that the egg isn't real. Avoid using the word *ordinary* to describe the ordinary. The audience can see what it is. Never underestimate their intelligence. Use it for your own gain.

Making something mechanical work requires no skill. So remember that you must also add handling, presentation, and acting ability to make it skillful. Without skill there can be no misdirection. There is a definite skill involved in simulating conditions that do not exist. For example, when you take an object and pretend to put it into the left hand from the right, the left hand must take the shape and must move as though the object were really there. A small ball will allow the hand to close tighter than a larger one. Simulation must imitate the false condition we set up. Consider also the dissimulation required to conceal the real facts with pretended ones. A little hiding of the truth goes far in the area of misdirection.

You can make a false picture real with a few simple verbal or facial expressions. Pretend to put the egg into the bag, then take a look into the bag and offer a nod convincing the spectator—"*Yep, still there.*" This can be done without saying a single word. A little suggesting both physically and orally can help carry off the ruse. Use every facility you have in taking the spectator down the garden path—timing, patter, facial expression, noise, and a little "lying." A loud noise on one side of a stage assisted Blackstone's helpers. They stole a cage full of ducks on the other side without being seen. So the ear can be deceived as easily as the eye. Ventriloquists will tell you this from experience. The vent figure is the visual misdirection as the vocal skill deceives the ear.

Your magic must be done before the spectator realizes you are doing it. Misdirection is the key. Study the tricks in this book and see how we have created our diversions. Watch other magicians and, if you don't watch too closely, you might catch them at the technique of handling and redirecting the minds of the audience.

MAKING THINGS DISAPPEAR

If you take one ball, or more, & seeme to put it into your other hand, and whilst you use charming words, you conveie them out of your hand into your lap; it will seeme strange. For when you open your left hand immediatlie, the charpest lookers on will saie it is in your other hand, which also then you may open; & when they see nothing there, they are greatlie overtaken.

Reginald Scot, DISCOVERIE OF WITCHCRAFT, 1584
Book XIII, Chapter

THE VANISH

"Can you make me disappear?" *"Can you make my wife disappear?"* . . . *"my boss? . . . my headache?"*

If you haven't heard those questions as yet, be prepared. As soon as anyone learns that you are interested in performing magic, he or she is sure to ask one or more variations of these questions. When you are asked, the answer is: *"Of course I can!"*

If the conditions are right, you can make anything disappear. After all, you *are* a magician. To cause something to disappear is merely to hide it from the spectators' view. But you will have to hide the object while the audience is watching. That is the magic part of it. The method you will use depends on one or more of the following four factors.

1. *The size and shape of the object.* If a person were to disappear, you would need a place to conceal him or her. Perhaps a large box or container. A smaller object will require a smaller hiding place.
2. *The setting.* If you are in a theater, you could use larger props. If you are at a dinner table, you would not be able to hide objects larger than the hiding places around the table.
3. *The props available.* In your act you can prepare the

props you need for the vanish. If you are asked for an
impromptu vanish, you must use the props at hand.

4. *The angle of vision of your spectators.* Where the spectator sits or stands will have a strong bearing on your
vanish. You will probably adjust your own position so
that the "disappearing" object is unseen.

To teach you how to vanish an elephant would be a most
impractical lesson for this book. It is more valuable to learn to
vanish objects that are familiar and available to you.

Let us begin with small objects and work our way up.

The French Drop

Obtain a coin, ring, sugar cube, dice, or similar small object. For
our example we will use a coin. The setting is standing up or
sitting down at any place where the audience is relatively close.
You will adjust the angle of vision so that the spectator is directly
in front of you or at your left. Seven steps to follow are:

1. Hold the coin in your left hand by its milled edge. Fig. 1

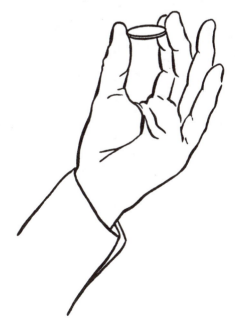

Fig. 1

shows the coin between the thumb and first two fingers above the first joint. If you relax the pressure of your thumb, the coin will fall into your cupped left palm.

2. Place the coin back into position again. Bring your right hand over the left, palm down. The right thumb goes under the coin. The tips of the right fingers above it. (Fig. 2.)

3. Take the coin from the left hand with the right thumb and first two fingers. Close the right hand and turn it palm up. Practice taking the coin this way a few times before you go on.

4. Now for the fun. This time you will not really take the coin away. You will pretend to take it. All the fingers will move exactly as they did when you really took the coin. As the right hand covers the left, the *left thumb will relax* and the coin will silently drop into the left cupped palm. The right fingers will close and *you will move the right hand away from your body, turning the palm up.*

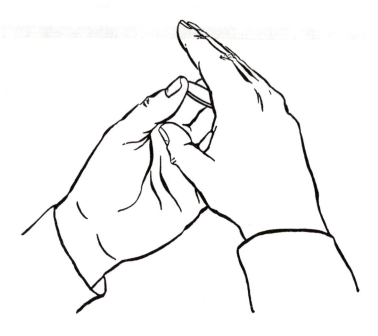

Fig. 2

5. The left hand, with its coin, will gently move to your left pocket. The hand will leave the coin in the pocket and then come out again, pretending to carry some invisible "woofle" dust with it.
6. Pretend to sprinkle the imaginary dust over the closed right fist. *"A little sprinkle of woofle dust will do wonders for this coin."*
7. Open the right hand by lifting one finger at a time from the pinky, ring finger, middle, and all the way open. *"It will make the coin disappear."*

Learn the seven steps above until you have them perfect. If you work in front of a mirror, you will see how the trick looks to your spectator. At the same time it will condition you not to look at your hands while you are doing the "dirty work." Always move the hands *slowly* and *naturally*. Any fast or unnecessary movement of the left hand will call attention to it. The trick begins after the coin is in your pocket. It is then that you create the magic. The acting ability and pretense of adding the "woofle dust" and the magical opening of your empty hand are most impressive to your audience.

The misdirection begins as soon as the right hand is closed. When you move your right hand away from your body, your eyes should follow it. When you speak, you will make reference to a coin that is no longer where the spectator thinks it is. When you say *"this coin,"* you can move the right hand up and down once. Pretend you believe that the coin is still there, and your audience will believe it as well. Practice!

Palming

"Palming" is the term we use for hiding an object in the hand. The object rests in the palm while the audience sees only the back of the hand. You can only palm objects that can be held in the hand without falling out. A small coin such as a dime or nickel falls out easily, so for them you would have to use the French Drop. A larger coin such as a quarter or half-dollar can be held by the muscles in the palm. Try this simple exercise.

Place a quarter or half-dollar in the palm of your right hand.

The object should rest at the base of the thumb (Fig. 3). Gently squeeze the muscles at the bottom of the pinky and thumb together. You will feel the pressure of the object. Now turn your palm over so that it faces the floor. The object should not fall out. Your hand may be in a cramped position, so try to correct it by relaxing the muscles very slightly. If the object falls, you have either relaxed too much, or it must have been in the wrong place. Experiment by moving the coin around in the palm until it is comfortable. Practice keeping an object in the palm position. Do other things, such as writing or picking up objects with your fingers, while a coin or bottle cap or ping pong ball is in this position. Any small object that fits in the palm will do. You will soon get the "feel" of palming that object. Palming is the most difficult thing to learn in doing sleight-of-hand magic. Once you master it with practice, you will have no trouble in making any small object disappear. Try various objects as you practice. Read the following

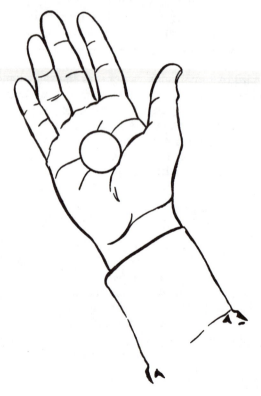

Fig. 3

description of the "classic" coin palm, but do not try it until you have the "feel" of palming.

Classic Palm Vanish

The position we just described is called the "classic" palm. Vanishing things by this method has been used by the master magicians from the earliest days of recorded magic.

Various shapes can be held in this manner. You can palm a pack of matches, a ping-pong ball, a cork, a pair of dice, a flash cube, a folded dollar bill, etc. How does the object get into the right position? The easiest way is to put it there in full view of your spectator. When you do so, you must not move the muscles immediately.

Here is how you should perform the vanish. Place the object in the right palm (the left palm if you are left-handed). Bring the other hand in front of you, palm up. The right hand will now turn in toward your body, at the same time contracting the muscles a bit. This will secure the object. The back of the right hand is seen by the audience. It is in a vertical position with the pinky going into the left hand, touching the base of the fingers. (Fig. 4.)

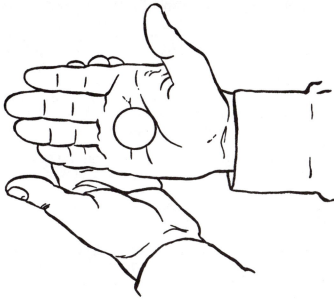

Fig. 4

Curl the left fingers in toward the back of the right hand. Move the right hand toward your body and then away to your right. The left fingers hide the empty, cupped left palm. Close the left hand.

It should appear as if you were placing the object from the right hand into the left hand. When you close the left hand, remember that it must look as if there is an object in it. Close the hand into a position that could hold the object. For example, you wouldn't be able to close it all the way if a ball were there.

Once again, misdirection is important. Move the left hand away from your right hand. The right hand can either rest alongside your body or can go to your pocket for the "woofle" dust, as it did in the French Drop vanish.

Classic Coin Vanish

A coin such as a quarter or half-dollar can be vanished from your fingertips with the "classic" palm. Here is how this is accomplished.

Place the coin flat on the tips of your middle and ring fingers (Fig. 5). Palm is flat in front of you. Turn the fingers of the hand to the left (counterclockwise), toward your body, so that the back of the hand now faces the audience and the fingertips face inward (Fig. 6). Push the coin up against the palm and into the "classic" position. The muscles will hold it there. Repeat the action of bringing the right hand over the left cupped palm as in the previous vanish. Close the left hand and move it to your left. Blow on the closed hand and open it gently, one finger at a time. The coin is gone.

Now for the subtle part. Turn your right and left hands so that the palms are almost directly in front of your face. The fingers are open (Fig. 7). The middle fingers are at a 45-degree angle in relation to the floor. The coin is in the hand and will not fall out at this angle. The spectator cannot see into the right palm. *"Gone"!*

Bring the left hand down and slap the right hand against it as if you were applauding. Applaud twice more, remove the right hand and stare at the left hand, where the coin mysteriously has reappeared.

"Hurray for the magician. He's done it again!"

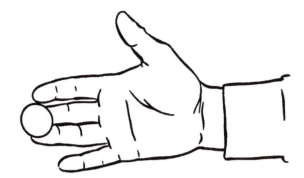

Fig. 5

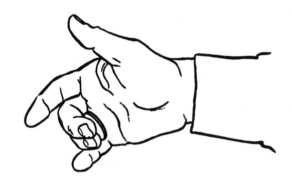

Fig. 6

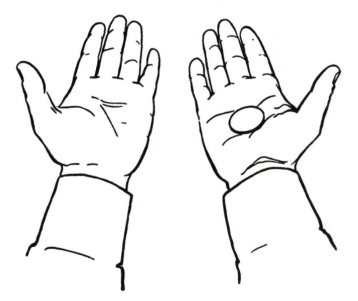

Fig. 7

Never Was

Once it has been established that you are a magician, the audience is conditioned to expect miracles. Using this knowledge, you can create an impossible vanish dependent solely on the spectator's expectation.

Ask your spectator if he or she has a "bunch" of small change. The wording is important. The victim will produce a small handful. Name any one of the coins you see duplicated. Let us assume you see a few dimes. *"Let's use this dime!"*

Reach into the pile of coins with your right hand. The fingers go into the pile and you pretend to take a coin. Take nothing. Hold the thumb and fingers pressed together as though you actually took one. Put the coin into the left hand as if it actually did exist. You must pretend and act as though it is really there. Close the left hand. The right hand turns palm up, and the right middle finger rubs the back of the left hand. This gesture tells the spectator you are not hiding anything in the right hand. Open both hands palms up and fingers apart. The coin is gone!

Since your spectator accepts you as a sleight-of-hand artist, he or she will assume that you made the coin disappear with great skill. The only risk that you run is that the spectator might ask for the money back. In this case it would cost you a dime. But it is worth it, I assure you. It is a small price to pay for a valued reputation.

You're Too Late

This is an impromptu coin vanish that can be mastered very easily. Use a quarter or a nickel. Using your right thumb, press the coin against your right leg about eight inches above the knee. (You will have to be wearing long pants or loose slacks.)

The right thumb will hold the coin in place while the left hand takes a position alongside the right hand. Both thumbs are side by side. The fingers of both hands pull some of the cloth back, turning the coin over toward your body, under the cloth. Your right thumb slides the coin back into the right hand as the left index finger covers the spot where the coin is supposed to be.

The coin is drawn away, hidden by the fingers of the right hand.

"Put your finger right here against the coin.

As the spectator reaches to do this, your left index finger moves away so that the cloth drops open, revealing that the coin is gone.

"You're too late!"

Put the right hand into the pocket and bring it out again with the coin.

"The coin went right through my slacks."

Practice this one a few times. You'll find that it is a fun vanish.

Table Sweep

A coin is the most popular of the small objects that the magician is asked to vanish. The diagram shows a coin, but you can also use bottle caps, sugar cubes, a pack of matches, a small paper ball, or any object that can be covered by your hand. Small objects can be vanished most effectively while you are seated at a table. Most closeup magicians work sitting down at a bridge table, where they can perform astounding feats with a Table Sweep Vanish. This is my own term for something magicians call *"lapping."* When you have progressed to advanced magic, you will find other methods and discover that "lapping" is an art all by itself. I will deal with this simple form.

Place the object to be vanished about six inches away from the edge of the table nearest you. You must be seated quite comfortably, with your feet on the ground and your knees together. If there is a space between your legs, it should be covered by a dinner napkin, handkerchief, or the cloth of your trousers. The elusive object will end up in your lap. What we don't want is a "clang" as it falls through your legs and onto the floor.

First consider the size and shape of the object. You have your setting, which is the table. Consider the angles of vision. The spectators can be sitting directly in front of you or, if you are at a small table, at your left or right—but *not* alongside of you. The sweep is performed easily. Reach for the object with your right hand. The hand must be placed in front of the object. Slide the object along the table and toward your body in a single contin-

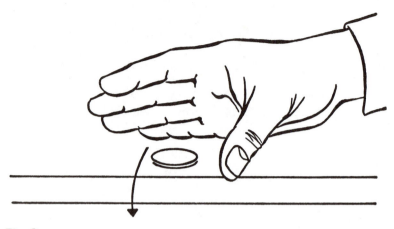

Fig. 8

uous motion. The object is literally swept off the table and into your lap. (Fig. 8.)

This action by itself would easily be seen. The acting and misdirection used here are important to focus attention on where the object is supposed to be going. You must use a bit of acting ability and pretend that you are picking the object off the table and setting it into the left hand. Bring your left hand forward along with your whole body the very moment the object reaches the end of the table. The right hand closes in the same manner as if the object were still in it. The fingers of the left hand receive the object and close around it. The vanish is apparently performed in the center of the table.

Your eyes are very important here. During the entire action your eyes must travel from a point directly in front of you to a position where you are watching the left hand. Your eyes move in the same direction the spectator must follow. Never look down.

Practice the Table Sweep with various small objects. Study the hands so that you can see what position each hand takes when it really lifts and receives the object. Watch how the right hand closes on the object, then mimic this without the object. Use the table sweep sparingly and with care for the proper angles and size of the object. Done smoothly, this can be most deceptive and will fool even the most knowledgeable audiences.

Back of the Hand

The following is a description of a vanish called the "back palm." The object isn't hidden in the palm at all. It is going to be concealed behind the hand. Use a small playing card or a business card for this one.

Hold the card by its shortest end so that the right thumb is in the middle, almost at the edge of the card. The middle and right ring fingers should be curled behind the card as in Fig. 9. The pressure of the thumb should be directly at the point where the two fingernails meet. If your index finger is extended slightly, it will help you for the next movement.

Clip the long edges of the card between the pinky and the second joint of the index finger. Bend those fingers back into your palm so that the two corners of the card are locked between them (Figs. 10, 11).

Extend the fingers to open your hand, and the card will vanish from the front and will be in a position in the back of the hand (Fig. 12).

Your angles are critical for this vanish. Practice with a mirror, which will be the audience. Turn your body to the right so that your left side is to the mirror. Hold the card in the proper position. Move your hand up and down in an arc a few times. Count to yourself, "One, two, three." At the count of three clip the card and vanish it by opening the hand. The mirror will reflect an apparently empty palm. Take a step forward and pluck the card from the air by reversing the procedure of the vanish (close your hand). While you rehearse, you will see that as you look into the mirror, you are watching the audience. Although your body is turned, your head is facing to the left. You will learn to perform the move without watching your hands. Do this for practice only, not as a trick. You are going to use this mostly to develop your own dexterity.

This vanish is a simple form of the more intricate stage technique of vanishing and producing cards from the air. Should you want to continue with this technique, there are many trade publications that deal with cards. With training and skill you can learn to vanish fans of cards and have them reappear singly from back palm position.

Many famous manipulators such as Cardini, Channing Pollack, Romaine, and Frank Garcia have made this technique a feature in their stage performances.

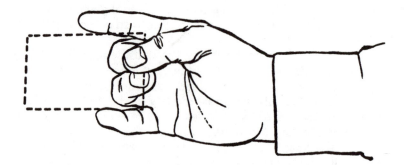

Fig. 9

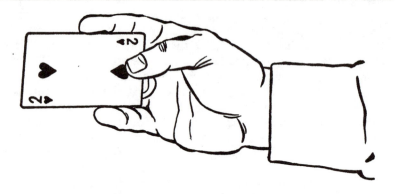

Fig. 10

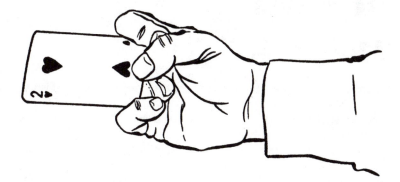

Fig. 11

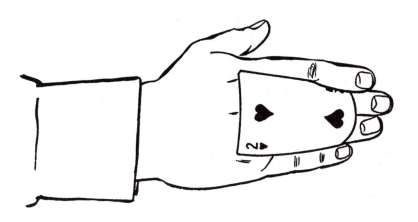

Fig. 12

33

MECHANICAL DEVICES

The Pull

Larger objects require more than just the hands to accomplish the vanish. The gimmick we are going to use here is called the "pull." This particular device was invented by a man named Buatier and was originally used to bring a handkerchief into the sleeve. Modern dress makes the sleeve a very impractical place to hide most objects. Buatier had a cord up one sleeve attached to his wrist. The other end traveled around his body and ran into the other sleeve. By pulling his right hand forward he drew the object into the left sleeve.

The pull we are going to use is an elastic device that will take the object away quickly and without a chance of being seen. The object will be hidden under your jacket or blouse. Various pulls are designed to accommodate different sizes and shapes of objects. Here is how to make a handkerchief pull.

You will need a 12-inch length of heavy elastic thread or cord. Attach a safety pin to one end with a few secure knots. Pass the other end of the elastic through the small ring at the back of another safety pin, but do not tie it. The loose end of the elastic will now be attached to a receptacle or cup that will hold a handkerchief. You can make this from an empty plastic film container such as is used for 35mm film. If you use a metal can, paint it black. Bore a tiny hole in the bottom of the can. Pass the end of the elastic through the hole and make a few sturdy knots so that it cannot come through the hole again (Fig. 13).

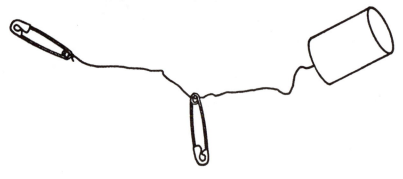

Fig. 13

Pin one end of the pull to the right side of your trousers or skirt just at waist level. Bring the pull around the small of your back toward your left side. Pin a second, loose safety pin to your trousers about five inches from the end of the cup. This pin is used to stop the pull from flying around the other side of your body. The cup will hang down from the second pin. You must wear a jacket or blouse to hide it. If the cup hangs below the bottom of your coat, move the loose pin to the left.

Here is how to use the pull. Turn your body to the left, so your right side is facing the audience. Have a small handkerchief available on a table at your left. Pick up the handkerchief with your right hand. At the same time your left hand will casually take the cup from under the coat. The attention is on the handkerchief, so don't worry about being seen.

Swing your whole body around to the right, so your left side is facing the audience. The cup will be hidden in the left hand and held there by the pinky and left ring fingers (Fig. 14). The elastic will be hidden as it is stretched along the left arm. Cup the left hand, wrapping the fingers around the gimmick. Push the center of the handkerchief into the small cup. It will appear that you are merely pushing the hanky into your left fist. Continue to tuck the handkerchief into the fist until it is completely out of sight.

Gently release the pressure of your fingers on the cup, and it will fly under the coat with a snap. Disregard the slight noise; it will not be heard by your audience. Try to keep your hand in the same cupped position. Pretend that the handkerchief is still in the hand as you turn to face your audience. Pull back your left sleeve a bit. Blow on the closed fist. Open the hand slowly to show that the cloth has vanished.

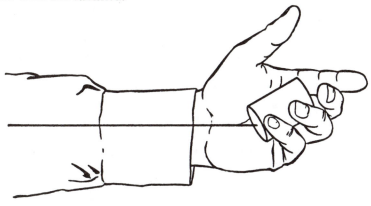

Fig. 14

More Pulls

Other pulls can be made by changing the receptacle. For example, you might use the top of a commercial ball point pen. In this case you would attach the top pin to the inside of your coat, up near the collar. The second pin would not be required. The pull would hang from the coat. Use a longer elastic. A lighted cigarette pushed into the cup would go out due to lack of air. The cigarette can be made to vanish the same way as the handkerchief.

Roll a dollar bill into the shape of a cigarette, push it into your hand, and it vanishes. Of course, it goes into the small cup that will accommodate its shape.

Try a pencil. Push one end into the receptacle, and cover the other end with your right hand. Pick up your knee and pretend that you are going to break the pencil in half. Let go of the cup as you lift your hands. Pretend to snap the pencil in half, then show both hands empty. With the pull hanging from the back of the coat, the length of the pencil will not be a problem.

Attach a small alligator clip to your elastic. As long as it can be hidden under the coat and will attach to the clip, any small object can be made to vanish quickly. If you don't want to make them yourself, pulls are available at magic and trick shops or in many commercial magic kits. There are handkerchief pulls, cigarette pulls, coin pulls, etc.

Down the Tube

Here is an interesting trick you can do with your handkerchief pull and a small paper tube. Use the empty tube from a toilet tissue roll. Cover it with a bright-colored contact paper or wrapping.

Place this prop on a table at your left. A small silk handkerchief and a wand or pencil are also on the table. Show your hands empty by rubbing them together a bit before you begin the trick.

Turn your body to the left and pick up the tube with your right hand. The left hand will secretly get the pull from behind your coat. This should be a casual gesture. Place the tube into the left hand so that it goes over the cup on the pull. The back of your right arm will cover the action for a moment. Now the right hand picks up the silk handkerchief. All eyes will be on the cloth as you turn to face the audience. Poke the middle of the handkerchief into the tube. Then take the wand or pencil and use it to push the

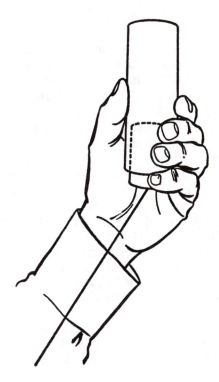

Fig. 15

silk hanky into the cup on the pull. It will appear that the hand-kerchief is going into the center of the tube (Fig. 15).

The right hand holds the wand up and to your right.

"Watch for a miracle."

As you say this, release the pull. The handkerchief will travel under the coat while all the eyes are on the wand. Your left hand holds an empty tube. Do not allow the end to be seen by the audience. Hold the tube so that they can only see the outside. Now lift the tube to your eye level. Pass the wand through the tube.

"The wand goes through the tube. This proves the handker-chief is gone."

The audience will not be fooled by that statement so you continue . . . .

"But for those of you who are skeptics. . . ."

Turn the tube and show that it is empty. Spin the tube around the wand a bit and then take your bow.

Amedeo's Vanish

Amedeo Vacca was a well-known comedy vaudeville magician who performed in the twenties. He was an advance man for Harry Houdini. A few years before he died, he divulged his method for coin and cigarette vanishes that he had been using for many years. His vanish was accomplished with a pull, but he added an extra something that fooled the most knowledgeable of magicians. Here is how he improved the method.

This time we will vanish a key. Prepare a pull by using a piece of elastic eight inches long. One end will have a small safety pin securely attached. The other end is knotted around a five-inch length of fine fishing line. (Two-pound nylon "platyl" line is very strong and works quite well.) A string of colorless nylon thread will also work. The purpose of using nylon is to make the connection invisible. The other end of the nylon will be tightly knotted to the small hole on top of your house key (Fig. 16).

This is one case where you will use your sleeve for a vanish. The flat shape of the key will not cause a bulge in the sleeve.

Attach the safety pin inside the sleeve of your jacket, just below the armhole. The key should hang about two or three inches from the end of the sleeve near your wrist. If it hangs too low, shorten the length of elastic or raise the position of the pin. If it hangs too high, lower the pin.

A moment before doing the vanish, you must obtain the key. You could place both hands behind your back and pull the key from the right sleeve with the left hand. The key will then be retained in the right hand, held by the middle finger and thumb. If you have a chance to do it without being seen, you can just pull it out and hold it in your hand until you are ready.

"Let me show you something interesting with a key."
Put your right hand into your right pocket and bring it out again.

Key   Catgut   Elastic   Pin

Fig. 16

This time allow the key to be seen in your fingers.

"May I borrow a handkerchief?"

If none is available, be prepared to use one of your own from a left pocket. Drape the handkerchief against your right leg so that one corner points up at you. This is done with the left hand. This corner is about three inches above your knee (Fig. 17). Set the key in the center of the handkerchief, holding it in place with the right middle finger. Spread your fingers apart. The nylon will run along the middle finger line and up to your wrist.

Hold the key in place with the left index finger. Turn the right hand by swiveling it to your right, palm up, then back to position again.

"This is my house key."

The right middle finger takes it again. This action allows the spectator to see the entire key for a second. The colorless nylon will

Audience view of handkerchief on knee

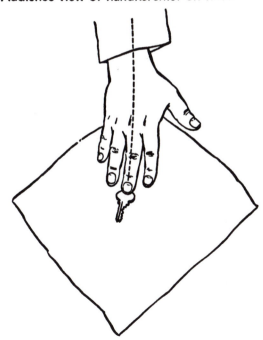

Fig. 17

not be visible against the white cloth.

Your left hand will now begin to fold the handkerchief so that one corner (#1) comes in toward the center of the cloth, covering the key. (Figs. 18, 19.) Follow the sequence as shown in the diagram, folding number one first, then number two, and finally number three from the bottom up. All this is done with the left hand.

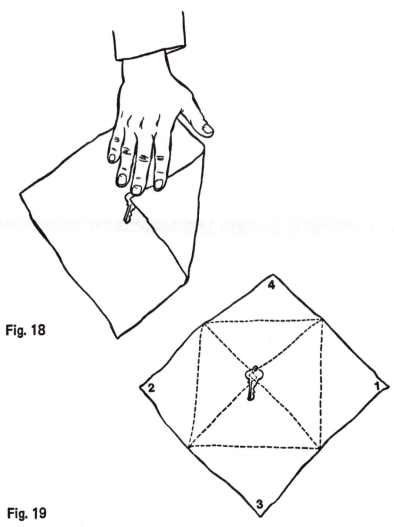

Fig. 18

Fig. 19

Gently lift the right hand to take the last top corner. The key will quietly shoot into the sleeve. Do not hesitate—continue the folding action, bringing the top corner down to make an envelope of the handkerchief. The left hand will lift the handkerchief off the knee with care as though it held the key.

"I keep my key wrapped in a handkerchief so that I can't lose it. Unless someone asks me to do some magic. Like this." Toss the hanky into the air with the left hand. Allow the right hand to catch one corner, bringing it down with a snap. The key is gone.

"I really don't need a key. My magic teacher told me that doing these miracles would open doors for me."

Amedeo always wore his "pull" and was ready for a quick vanish whenever he was asked to perform impromptu. He used a coin with a small hole drilled at the top to take a catgut thread. The modern use of nylon line allows for free handling of the pull, since it cannot be seen as easily as elastic. If you can rig your pulls with the extra nylon piece, the connection is almost invisible. This will allow you to vanish objects almost straight on without the need of turning the body too much.

Lightning Bill Vanish

Money magic is always very popular with audiences. The prop is readily available in anyone's pocket, and when you borrow his money, the spectator will surely be interested in keeping a close eye on what you are doing.

This vanish requires an unknown helper called a "feke." The prop is made from a standard-sized man's handkerchief. Select a white one that has a wide hem around the border. You will also require a piece of white paper cut to the size of a dollar bill (2-1/2 x 6 inches). Roll the paper tightly into a small, two-and-half-inch package. Seal the open end with cellophane tape. Open the hem of the handkerchief by cutting the thread on one end. Insert the paper tube into the hem and resew it. Your "feke" is

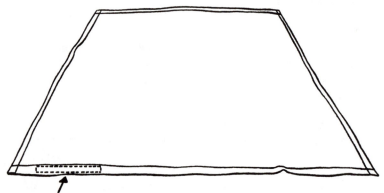

Rolled paper sewn in hem

Fig. 20

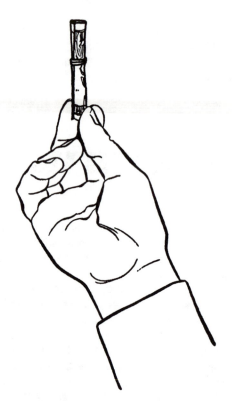

Fig. 21

now ready to use. Keep your gimmicked handkerchief in any left-hand pocket (Fig. 20).

Borrow a dollar bill from a spectator. Roll it into a small package as you did with the paper. Snap a small rubber band around the bill so that it does not unroll. Hold this at one end by the right thumb and middle finger (Fig. 21).

The left hand finds the handkerchief and shakes it open. Hold it by any one of the ungimmicked corners. The right hand takes the gimmicked corner, pressing it between the index finger and the rolled bill. It will be easy to find the gimmicked corner since the weight of the package will cause it to tip slightly. Bring this corner and its bill underneath the handkerchief to the center of the cloth. The left hand will let go of its corner and grasp the gimmicked end through the top of the cloth. The right fingers pull the real bill back into the right hand.

"We'll need another rubber band. Can you hold this bill, please?"

As you say this, hand the spectator the parcel; he takes the gimmicked end as your right hand goes to your right pocket. Leave the bill there. The spectator will feel a small parcel under the cloth and assume that he is holding the bill.

Your right hand comes out of the pocket empty.

"I don't have another rubber band, so let's forget the whole thing. You may let go."

As you say this, grab any loose corner of the handkerchief and snap it out of the spectator's hand. Open the cloth and show it by holding one corner in each hand. If your crisscross your hands in front of you, you can show both sides.

"I'll do this trick again. Next time we'll use a hundred-dollar bill."

This vanish is a very good one.

Satan's Cloth

Anything unexplained in ancient times, such as magic, was usually thought to be the work of the devil. This vanish uses a simple but devilish little prop. In effect, a large napkin or kerchief is shown and folded into a bag. An object is dropped into the bag. On opening the cloth, the object is seen to have disappeared.

You will need two identical neckerchiefs or pieces of cloth about 16 inches square. The exact measurements are not critical,

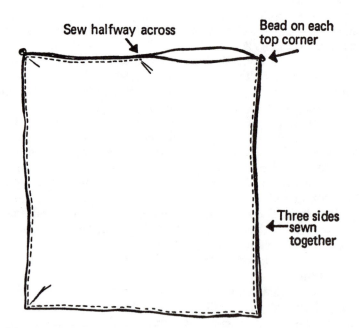

Sew halfway across

Bead on each top corner

Three sides ←sewn together

Fig. 22

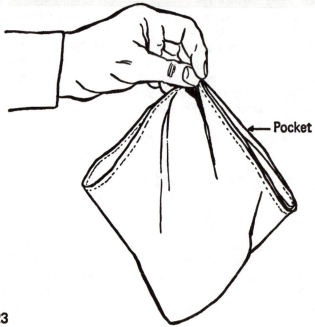

Pocket

Fig. 23

but be sure that both squares are the same size. A patterned piece of broadcloth or sturdy cotton is recommended. Dark colors are better than light shades, and the more design printed on the cloth, the better.

Place one square directly on top of the other. Sew three of the edges together, forming a bag. Now sew the top sections together only halfway across. You will have a large opening on one side of the bag. Sew a small bead on each of the two top corners of the bag—one near the opening, the other on the opposite closed side (Fig. 22). You can hold the cloth open by taking a bead between the thumb and index fingers of each hand. In this position the top opening is at your right and the cloth looks like a single kerchief.

Here is how to fold the cloth for the vanish. Bring each corner up into the left hand and hold it between the thumb and index finger (Fig. 23). Holding all four corners creates a bag. Your right hand will now open the secret pocket. It will look like a simple adjustment of the cloth. Do not call attention to this movement. The right hand picks up the object you wish to vanish and drops it into the open pocket. Bring both hands together where all four corners meet. The right hand takes one bead, the left hand takes the other. The beads are held between the thumbs and index fingers. As your hands come apart, drop the other two ends. The item has disappeared! You may notice a slight bulge, depending upon the size and shape of your object. Don't worry about it. A heavily patterned cloth will mask the bulge.

Show both sides of the cloth by crisscrossing your hands in front of one another.

To reproduce the object, fold the bag as before and reach into the secret pocket with the right hand. You will find the missing item without too much trouble.

Practice working with the Satan Cloth. Here is a fun trick you do with a deck of cards and the cloth. Secretly have four aces on top of your deck. Make the small bag and then pick up the deck. The right hand will push the top four cards into the folds of the bag. Then the rest of the cards are dropped in small groups into the pocket section. Hold the cloth over a table. Open the cloth and the deck will have vanished, leaving four aces to flutter to the table.

The Satan's Cloth is quite versatile and can vanish eggs, balls, oranges, etc. Use your imagination. In the event that you do not want to make your own prop, you can purchase the cloth commercially. It will be called a Devil's Hank or a Devil's Napkin.

Paper Bag Vanisher

Ribbons, cards, string, silk handkerchiefs, or other lightweight objects can be vanished with the use of a simple paper bag prop you can make at home. A silk handkerchief is perfect since it can be crumpled up into a tiny package.

You will need two identical paper bags. Their size will depend on what you want to vanish. Open one of the bags and cut the entire front side off with a sharp scissors (Fig. 24). Apply some glue or rubber cement to the bottom and side flaps. Place this cut bag into another bag. The rear wall of the cut bag should be about half an inch away from the rear wall of the regular bag. You can vary the distance depending on the space you need to accommodate the object. For a silk handkerchief a half-inch is fine.

Press the bottom and sides, firmly cementing them to the outer bag. When they are dry, you will have a divider in the bag (Fig. 25). The smaller of the two compartments will be used for the vanish. Fold the bag and place it on your table.

To show the bag empty, pick it up and open it, pressing the rear wall and the divider together with the right hand. The left hand holds the opposite wall. Lift the bag so that the audience can look inside. They cannot see the divider.

"What do you see in the bag?"

Wait for a reply.

"Nothing? That's what I'm getting you for your birthday. Nothing!"

Push a small silk handkerchief into the back compartment. Shake the bag a bit.

"What color was the handkerchief?"

Wait for a reply.

"Wrong! It has no color. The reason for that is . . . that it isn't!"

Place both hands on the front panel of the bag, thumbs inside, fingers outside. Tear the front panel in half, pulling the paper away from you. The silk handkerchief has vanished! Crumple the paper into a ball and toss it aside where no one can pick it up. Remember to retrieve it after the performance so you can get your handkerchief back.

The Paper Bag gimmick has many other uses, such as producing or switching objects. We will discuss this later.

Glue shaded sides and
under bottom section

Fig. 24

1/2 inch space

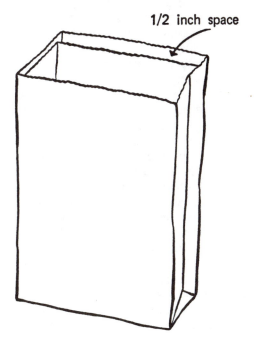

Fig. 25

SOMETHING FROM NOTHING

How to pull laces innumerable out of your mouth, of what colour or length you list, and never anie thing seene to be therein.

Reginald Scot, DISCOVERIE OF WITCHCRAFT, 1584
Book XIII, Chapter XXXII

THE PRODUCTION

Pulling rabbits from empty hats seems to be the trademark of the magician. Nobody knows exactly where the idea originated, but the trick was popular in the early 1800s. Earlier street magicians used hats as a natural object since they could not carry large props. A hat was always available, and it proved to be a good place to hide things. Modern magicians no longer wear fancy top hats, and so they produce things from boxes, tubes, bags, and other seemingly empty containers. When you produce something from nothing, this is called a Production.

The production is most often accomplished by the same means as the vanish. You merely reverse the procedure. Instead of placing an object into a container for the vanish, you have one secretly hidden there and remove it from its hiding place. When you put a silk handkerchief into an empty paper bag, it is hidden by the secret pocket and you can show the bag empty again. This is the vanish. Conceal the handkerchief there in the first place, show the bag empty, and pull the cloth from its hidden pocket. Voila! A Production.

In outlining the various methods used for producing things, we must again consider the size and shape of the object, the audience's view, and the surroundings. Once we have decided that we are going to produce something special, we must now select the proper hiding place.

Where to Hide Things

Picture the magician walking out onto the stage. He raises his hand and plucks a playing card out of the air. How did he do it? We know now that objects can be hidden in the hands or behind them. A card that started in back-palm position can be produced merely by reversing the vanishing process. A group of cards can be back-palmed and produced one at a time with proper handling.

A small ping-pong ball can be produced by concealing it in the classic palm position. Pick up an empty hat with one hand and reach into it with the other hand. If the ball is in the classic palm position, the audience sees the back of the hand. Pretend that you found it in the hat and take it out, reversing the vanish procedure once again.

You can see the similarities of the method when it comes to small objects. But how about bigger things?

The object that you intend to produce from a container is called a "load." The section that hides the object from view is called the "load chamber." Your load can be a rabbit, some silk handkerchiefs, a bottle of soda, or even a bowling ball (produced by comedy magician Johnny Thompson). The size of the load chamber is determined by the size of the object.

Let's Have a Drink

The Paper Bag Vanisher described earlier is a fine production prop for things like playing cards, dollar bills, silk handkerchiefs, or ribbons. The secret pocket can hide flat items. You could also use the Satan Cloth for producing an egg, ball, deck of cards, or even a baby chick.

Here is how you would produce a small glass of liquid from a Satan Cloth. Use a small shot glass half full of colored soda. Now wedge a rubber ball into the top of the glass so that the liquid will not spill even if the glass turns upside down. Drop this into the load chamber and leave the cloth on your table.

When ready for the performance, pick up the cloth by the two small beads. The bulky glass will be closest to your body. Crisscross your hands so the audience sees both sides of the cloth.

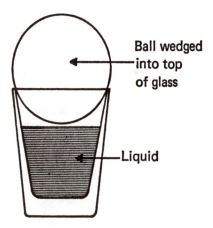

Ball wedged
into top
of glass

Liquid

Fig. 26

Bring the four corners together so you can hold them in one hand.
Your other hand reaches into the secret pocket and starts to bring
the glass up. When the glass is right side up, push off the ball so
that it will fall into the cloth again. Bring out the glass. Drink the
liquid and set the glass aside. Now shake out the cloth by holding
it at the two beads again. The ball is not seen, and the cloth appears
to be empty again. (Fig. 26.)

The Candy Bag

This very practical prop works the same way as the Paper Bag
Vanisher. It cannot be torn apart, but has the advantage of accom-
modating a larger, bulkier load. We are going to make a double bag
using three pieces of cloth each 7 x 9 inches. The cloth should
be much sturdier than the Satan's Cloth. Experiment with
a few different types until you find one that is pliable in your
hands, yet stiff enough to conceal a bulge. A plaid or heavily
patterned design is advisable. If you use a solid color, make it dark
blue or black.

   Have someone sew all three pieces together on only three
sides, to form a bag. The top opening should be seven inches wide.
For better handling and a showy piece of equipment use a contrasting ribbon to trim the top edges. A black bag with a red edge
makes a flashy appearance. When you look down into the bag, you
will see two compartments. This utility bag can be used for switching or vanishing objects as well as for the production we will describe. (Fig. 27.)

Middle wall creates
two compartments

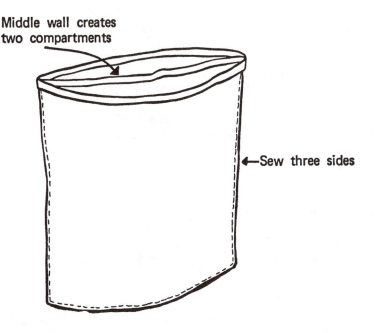

←—Sew three sides

Fig. 27

Fill one of the compartments with wrapped candies or lollipops.
Have this prepared on your table before the beginning of the trick.

*"When I was a small child, I saw a magician who really per-
formed great miracles. He used an empty bag very much like
this one. . . ."*

Pick up the bag by placing four fingers of your right hand
into the empty compartment. Your thumb is on the outside of the
cloth. Press the center compartment toward your thumb, hiding
the load trapped between the two walls. Your left hand will go
into the empty compartment and turn the bag inside out. The
right hand should not help in this procedure, as you must make
sure none of the candy falls out.

Once the bag is inside out, the left hand can go into the bag
again, spreading the fingers apart. This opens the bag better. Now
reverse the procedure and turn the bag right side out again.

Try to be as natural as possible and do not cause suspicion by being overcautious as the bag turns.

"The magician made a pass over the bag like this."

Remove the right hand and use it to gesture a bit. Now reach in and remove one or two pieces of candy.

"And he found candy inside." Now turn the bag inside out and back again, as before. *"Each time the made a pass, more candy appeared."* Produce a few more pieces. Then show the bag empty again by turning it as before.

"And that's why I learned magic. It was so impressive, and it ensures that I'll always have food to eat."

Turn the bag the proper way again, and pull out or dump out the rest of the load. When doing this, press the middle wall against the empty section with the left hand so that the load will drop out easily.

"Even if it's only candy."

It Pays to Advertise

A prop that does not look like a prop is above suspicion. In this case we will use a prop made from an ordinary tabloid newspaper. Lay one double sheet on a table. Fold a silk handkerchief or a lightweight scarf into a small parcel that is relatively flat. We don't want too much bulk. Set the parcel in the center of the right-hand side of your double sheet (Fig. 28).

Apply rubber cement or paper glue to the four sides of the right-hand page of the paper, as shown. Cut a single page from another double sheet of newspaper. Carefully set this page on top of the cement so that you will seal the handkerchief into the center of the paper. This is a double wall that will look natural.

Add a few more double sheets to the center of your gimmick, and the paper will look whole again. It can be freely handled when dry. You will open a few pages as you patter.

"A newspaper is a very important part of our daily lives. For example if you get on a bus, you can always sit on it to keep your pants clean. You can fold it and use it as a pillow to sleep on, on the way to work. You can wrap your lunch or swat a fly with a newspaper."

Remove the gimmicked sheet and toss the rest of the paper aside.

"I always do my shopping with the paper."

Fold the double sheet in half so that the thicker side is toward your body. Now fold the paper in half again by bringing the

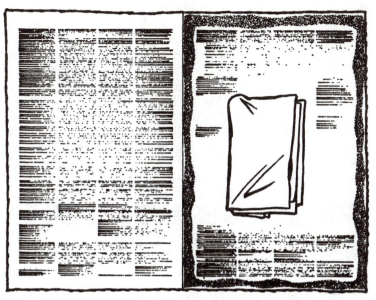

Handkerchief folded in center
Glue shaded areas.

Single sheet glued to
seal handkerchief in place.

Fig. 28

bottom section up away from you as you do so.

"It's my sister's birthday next week, and I found a great ad for silk scarves. She loves them. This is how a magician does his shopping. Find what you like, then get a magic wand...."
Use a wand or the rubber tip of a long pencil.

"And voila.... She gets her gift."
Push the pencil or wand through the center of the paper from behind. The silk scarf should pop right through the paper. Pull the scarf out gently and crumple the paper with the other hand. You can use the scarf for another trick.

BOXES AND TUBES

Mirror Box

Trapdoors, secret panels, mirrors, hidden wires, and threads have all been associated with the magician's production box. Such means were used in one form or another by magicians in years past. They were employed in various kinds of large, theater illusions in the days when technology was not as advanced as it is today. Only a few of yesteryear's magic gimmicks have survived. One of the props that is still used is the Mirror Box. Instead of being a theater prop it has become a more practical, club-sized box.

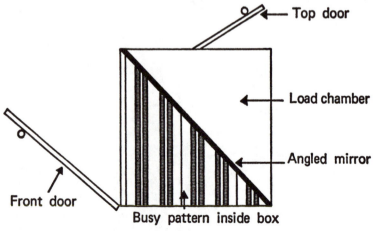

Fig. 29

The box is square and has a mirror angled from the bottom rear to the top front section (Fig. 29). When the front door is opened, the audience sees the mirror that is reflecting the same pattern as the bottom of the box. This is usually an overall or striped design to confuse the eye. The reflection also offers some depth so that the box appears to be empty. Only the front section is seen, the load chamber is out of sight behind the mirror. The magician has access to the load through a small door on top of the box. There are many versions of this box sold commercially. These are made of wood, plastic, or cardboard. If you intend to make your own mirror box, use a heavy cardboard. A good glass mirror is the best to use, although a thin sheet of mylar will work. If you use the mylar, make sure that it is mounted on a stiff piece of cardboard to prevent your load from distorting the mirror from behind.

Tip-over Box

This one works automatically. You can show the box empty by lifting the lid to allow the audience to see inside. When the front

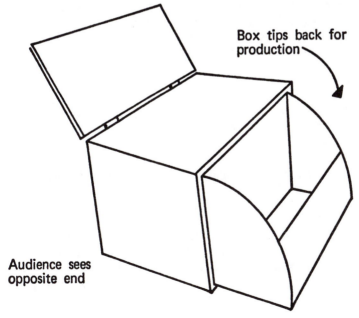

Box tips back for
production

Audience sees
opposite end

Fig. 30

lid is lifted, all they can see is the back wall of your load chamber. Study the illustration to see how cleverly this is designed. The load never moves; it rests behind the box on the table.

When the entire box is tipped backward, the lid becomes the top of the box. What was the back wall now becomes a side wall. The load is at the bottom of the box where it was all the time.

The parts are hinged together to allow the sections to tip. If you can picture a very large tip-over box, you can see how easy it would be to produce a person from inside. (Fig. 30.)

Tube of Plenty

Here is a production prop that can be seen at relatively close range without chance of detection. You can make this from a heavy cardboard mailing tube or you can fashion it out of oak tag. The principle is a simple one.

If you are using oak tag, cut one piece into a sheet 10 x 12 inches. Roll this into a tube 12 inches in length. Seal the sides with colorless or clear cellophane tape. Later you can decorate the outside with contact paper.

Make a second tube using a 10-inch-square piece of oak tag. You must taper the bottom of the smaller tube so that it almost resembles a cone (Fig. 31). The smaller tube will be set inside the larger one (Fig. 32). The wide ends are both the same circumference and must be taped together so that both tubes will look like only one.

Since the bottom of the inside tube is tapered, you are creating a false perspective. When someone looks into the wide end, it will appear to have its normal depth and shape. You will have enough space between the walls of the two tubes to hide several silk handkerchiefs, a length of ribbon, or some folding paper flowers if they are available. You might also consider using a small roll of confetti streamer.

Present you effect as follows: Show the wide side of the tube, handling it very casually, as though you were not trying to hide anything. Make sure that the narrow, faked end is toward your body. Bring the tube up to your eye level and look through it. Turn the tube from side to side, allowing the audience to look inside. If you have a long wand, you can help the illusion by pushing it through the tube from the back to the front.

Use two sheets of tissue paper about five or six inches square. Set one sheet on top of the faked end and secure it with a rubber

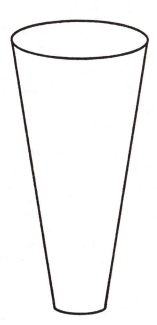

Fig. 31

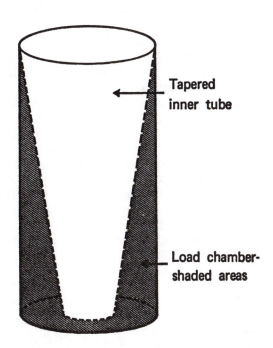

Tapered
inner tube

Load chamber-
shaded areas

Fig. 32

band. The outer opening is completely covered. Do the same with the second sheet, covering the front opening. If you wish, you could shine a flashlight through the back of the tube. The audience will see the light through the tissue.

Set the wider front end on the palm of your left hand. The right fingers poke a small hole in the tissue paper. Gently remove the silks or ribbons from the load section. When you get to the very last silk hanky, pull it up slightly, then push it into the center tube. Push it through the center with a wand so that it will break the front tissue and you can pull the hanky from the front of the tube. Casually show the tube before putting it away.

Professional magicians use one or more variations of this tube. The most popular ones are the Phantom Tube and the Genii Tube. These are usually made of metal and have much larger load chambers for producing more items.

And a Glass of Milk

You can produce a glass of milk from the Tube of Plenty. You will need a small plastic glass that can fit around the sides of the inner tube. Carefully cut out the bottom of the glass and paint the inside with a white acrylic paint—the same type as you might use for painting plastic models. Paint it to resemble an almost-full glass of milk. Do not paint it all the way up.

When the glass is thoroughly dry, set it inside the load end of your tube mouth first. Add a few silks, tucking them into the space that is left. The glass and tube are now ready for your production.

Go through all the steps of your production as you did in the previous trick. After the last hanky is produced, remove the rubber bands and paper. Make sure that you do not expose the back end of the tube while you do this. Now show the tube empty again by holding it at eye level.

Set the load section of the tube directly on your left palm. The left thumb and pinky firmly grip the glass. The right hand now pulls the tube directly up and reveals the glass on your palm. Pick up the glass, setting it on the table with your right hand very carefully as though you really had a full glass of milk.

Milk Through

In this variation you will use a real plastic glass that should fit into the bottom of your Tube of Plenty. First, tuck a few ribbons or streamers into the load area around the inner tube. Make sure that you leave some room for the glass.

Push the glass, mouth first, into the load area. But in this case you cannot show the tube empty, as you did before. This is what you must do.

Show a white handkerchief and drape it over your open left palm.

"We will use a white handkerchief for this miracle."

Set the tube on top of the open cloth so that the faked side is facing the palm. Grab the outer tube through the cloth and turn the tube toward the audience. They will see the inside, and although they cannot see clear through, it will look empty. The white cloth will hide the tint of the glass. (Fig. 33.)

"The reason that I use a white handkerchief is so that it will be the same color as the milk in this pitcher."

Show a small pitcher of milk. There must be enough milk in the

Fig. 33

pitcher to fill the glass three-quarters full. Test this before you set up the trick.

>*"When I pour the milk through the tube, it will not ruin the color of the handkerchief."*

Carefully pour the milk through the center of the tube. Try not to spill milk on the sides of the tube if it is made of cardboard.

>*"The milk does not spill or pass through the handkerchief. You might say that this is magic. Wrong! It is logic. The milk goes into a glass."*

Grab the glass through the handkerchief with the left hand. The right hand pulls the tube straight up to reveal the glass. Pretend to answer someone's question,

>*"Where did I get the glass? Oh, that was magic. Let me show you some more magic."*

Set the milk aside, show the tube empty, and cover it with the tissue so that you can proceed with a further production of goodies. If you are using a confetti streamer, pull one end and then turn the tube upside down. The confetti will pour out of the bottom very dramatically. Wind it with a wand for a pretty effect.

Out of the Hat

If you were asked to draw a picture of a magician, you would probably show him pulling a rabbit out of a tall top hat. No one seems to know when this trick was first performed, but magicians have been associated with it for many years. Modern magicians rarely pull rabbits out of hats. Street magicians used hats for centuries. A hat was always available for a production. In the 1800s magicians wore full-dress clothing and carried the topper, which was a good place to hide a load. Stage magicians of that period used the hats to bake cakes in their bowls, pass wands through the cloth and produce silks and ribbons and perhaps a rabbit. French magician Louis Comte produced his small baby son from a top hat.

It is obvious to us that anything that is produced from a hat must have been hidden inside the hat in the first place. When using his own, the stage magician often employed a "trick" hat, which had two compartments inside. The divider panel was hinged on top so that a flap would move from one side to the other. The load was covered on one side by a black flap. When shown empty, the hat was shown quickly, and the audience saw the black flap

Hinged flap moves from side to side.

Fig. 34

inside. The magician would then move the flap and pull the load items from within. (Fig. 34.)

The most spectacular effects were done with hats borrowed from members of the audience. We will work with a borrowed hat.

Milk and Cookies

I am a firm believer in using ordinary objects for your props. A borrowed hat and some kitchen items will be above suspicion for this effect.

Buy a 12-ounce can of baking soda. You can actually use any 12-ounce can, but you will have to relabel it to read "Baking Soda" or "Flour."

Remove the contents by cutting off the *bottom*, not the top of the can. Do this with a good can opener so that you have a smooth edge. Ragged edges will snag or scratch your skin.

Carefully cut a small hole about the size of a quarter in the back of the can, away from the front label. You will also need a small plastic glass that will fit easily inside the bottomless can. The glass will serve as your load chamber. Fill it with several kinds of small cookies. (For other productions you can also use silk ribbons, candies, rope, cards, etc.)

Set the glass, mouth up, on the table. Cover it with the can so that the label faces the audience. Get a small pitcher of milk, an egg, a package of sugar, and a salt shaker. Seal the inside cap of the salt shaker with some clear cellophane tape so that no salt can spill through the holes.

Borrow a hat and make a big fuss over it.

"It looks like a very expensive hat. I'll be careful not to spoil the shape."

Make sure that everyone can see that the hat is real. Turn up the brim and hold the hat like a bowl in your left hand. Pick up the can and the glass with the other hand. If you put your thumb into the hole in back of the can, you can press the glass to one side and easily pick up both of them together. Set the whole can into the hat as you speak.

"I once saw a magician baking cookies in a hat just like this one. I think he put some baking soda in the hat. . . ."

Put the can inside and leave it there for a moment. Then, on second thought, remove the can, leaving the glass and its load secretly inside. Make sure that you do not expose the bottom of the can as you set it back onto the table.

"No, the baking soda came later. It was salt."

Set the hat on the table so no one can see inside. Pick up the salt shaker and pretend to sprinkle salt into the hat. The holes are sealed, so don't worry. Roll up your sleeve and show that your hand empty as you place it into the hat. Use a wand and pretend to mix it a bit with the other hand. While your hand is in the hat, tip the glass on its side and spill the cookies into the hat. Remove your hand and pretend to taste the salt.

"Not enough salt!"

Pretend to sprinkle more salt into the hat. Now put your hand in again and set the glass so that it stands up inside the center of the hat, mouth up. Pretend to taste the salt when your hand comes out of the hat.

"Needs some sugar."

Tear the package and actually pour the sugar into the hat, but make sure it goes into the glass. This is the first real thing the spectators will see going into the hat. It will convince them that you are doing what you say you are.

"Now for some eggs. Maybe just one!"

Break your egg carefully so that it goes into the glass. Toss the shells in, too, for extra laughs.

"Don't worry about your hat, sir. I've done this before. Of course, I didn't use a real hat, last time I used a bowl. Now we'll need some milk."

Carefully pour a little bit of milk into the glass.

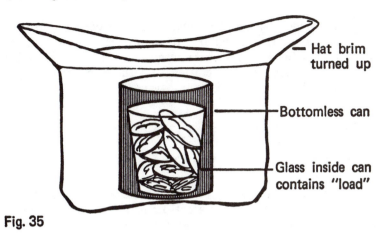

Hat brim turned up

Bottomless can

Glass inside can contains "load"

Fig. 35

"What did I forget? Oh yes, the baking soda."
Pick up the can, tipping it forward so that no one can see the missing bottom. Set the can over the glass and leave it in the hat. Wave a wand over the hat. Look inside.

"Looks great . . . messy, but great. Too much baking soda."
Remove the baking soda can and the glass by pressing the glass against the side as before, through the hole. Place both to one side away from the hat, where no one can touch it later. Pick up the hat in both hands and slowly walk away from the table. Act as if there were a liquid inside and you were afraid it would spill.

"I think it needs some cooking."
Remove a cigarette lighter from your pocket and pass it quickly under the hat. Make sure the flame is far away from the bottom of the hat.

"That's it! Cookies for everyone!"
Pass the hat into the audience, allowing everyone to have a cookie. Return the hat to its owner.

Be prepared with an extra hat on your stage in the event that no one lends you one. (Fig. 35.)

Black Art

A dead-black object placed in front of another dead-black object becomes invisible. The eye cannot make out the shape or outline of the object since there is no shadow or contrast. Magicians make good use of this knowledge.

The black-art principle is used in magic to hide objects. If you have a black backdrop on stage, you can dress a person in black and he or she would not be seen on the stage. A black thread cannot be seen against the magician's black tuxedo. Some very unusual effects can be created with the black-art principle. We are going to describe a production using it.

The Drinks Are on the House

You will need a small cardboard box with the top and one side cut away, so that you have only a bottom and three sides. The box should be high enough to hold a small bottle of soda or beer. Line the inside of the box with dead-black felt material. Glue it in so that there are no wrinkles or ripples in the cloth. Now glue some felt around the back of a small bottle so that exactly half the neck and body are covered from top to bottom. The front of the bottle has the label and name clearly showing.

Set the bottle in the center of the box so that the black side faces the audience. From a short distance the bottle cannot be seen and the box will appear to be empty. To ensure the illusion

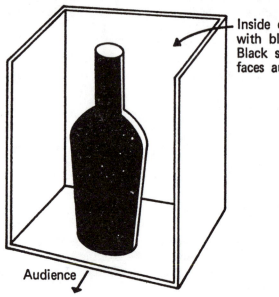

Inside of box lined with black felt. Black side of bottle faces audience.

Audience

Fig. 36

make certain that there are no lights directly on top of the box. No light must be shining into the box. This box should be on the center of a table, well backstage.

Here is how to make the bottle appear. Use a large foulard or cloth with a colorful print design—24 or 36 inches square would be fine. Hold the cloth, with one corner in each hand, by the thumb and index finger. If you crisscross your hands in front of you, both sides of the cloth can be seen. Now walk back to the box. Crisscross the hands again, but this time leave the right-hand corner draped over the left elbow. The entire cloth will be over the left arm. This conceals the right hand for a moment. During this quick interval the right hand must go into the box and turn the bottle so that it faces the front of the box. The audience cannot see anything since the cloth is in front of the box. If the left arm moves over the box, the entire cloth may be draped over the box.

Walk away from the box and get a small drinking glass. Make a magical gesture toward the box and snap the cloth away. The bottle will pop into view. If there is liquid in it, you can pour it into the glass gently, making sure the audience does not see the black felt on the back.

With some ingenuity you can vary the trick by using larger or smaller boxes and objects to fit. (Fig. 36.)

That's All, Folks!

Let's use the title of this trick to help us say "goodnight" or "so long" to our audience at the end of the act. Here is a novel way to use a production as a closing trick. We will use black art to create the effect.

We'll need two sheets of black construction paper. You will note that one side is duller than the other. Fold one sheet exactly in half horizontally, so that the dullest tones are on the inside of the fold. Glue a white 4-by-6-inch index card on the second sheet of construction paper. The duller side should be showing on the back of the index card when you are through. Trim the excess paper around the white card. Blacken the four white edges of the card with a black felt-tip marking pen.

Write the words, "That's All, Folks," in bold letters on the white face of the card. Place this sign inside the folds of the first sheet of paper.

To produce the sign you will pick up the folded paper with

Fig. 37

the right hand. Press the white side of the sign against the black top section of the paper (Fig. 37). This is held with the thumb. The audience sees the back of the sheet when you unfold it. Now bring your right hand down for a moment to allow the audience to see the other side. They cannot see the sign against the black paper. Fold the paper in half and place your left index finger inside the fold. The left thumb and index finger hold the sign. Release the top section, and the sign will suddenly come into view. Separate it from the other sheet so the audience sees two distinct pieces of paper, black and white.

PRODUCING MONEY

Magicians have been using money for their tricks since coins were first minted around 600 B.C. The idea of producing cash has always fascinated audiences. The Miser's Dream is the popular name for the trick that dates back to the 1800s. The routine was modernized by T. Nelson Downs, who was known as the "King of Koins," in about 1890. Mr. Downs reached into the air and plucked silver coins from nowhere, dropping them into his high silk hat. The hat was lined with a brass plate so that the coins were heard as they fell. Other vaudeville magicians of that era soon copied the effect, varying it with buckets and glass bowls instead of hats and by ending the routine with dollar bills. Various magicians presented the effect under different titles—"Coin Catching," "Aerial Mint," "Aerial Treasury," etc. Robert-Houdin called it the "Shower of Money." It was presented until 1975 by the late Al Flosso, who used it as a feature in his comedy magic act, pulling coins from behind the ears of the little boys he called on-stage. Before learning the routine, we must learn a basic move.

The Downs Palm

This is one of many sleights developed by T. Nelson Downs. Use a quarter or half-dollar. Hold the coin between the first joints of the index and middle fingers of the right hand as in Fig. 38.

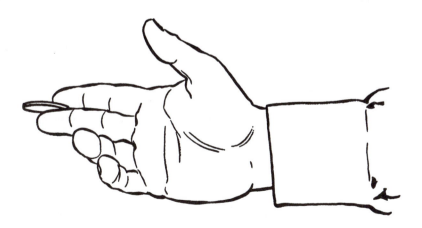

Fig. 38

Fig. 39

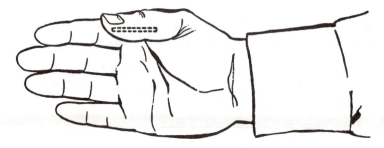

Fig. 40

Bend your fingers back into the crotch of the thumb so that the milled edge rests in the curve. Release the fingers and open the hand. The coin will remain hidden in the curve held only by the inside of the thumb (Figs. 39 and 40).

Keep the coin in this position for a while so that it becomes natural for you. If you swing your arm to the right, away from your body, the audience can see the palm of your hand with the coin hidden from their view.

Point to an imaginary spot to your left and reach toward that spot. By curling the index and middle fingers, reversing the basic steps, you can retrieve the coin to produce it. To make it more visible, push the coin upward with the thumb so the audience sees the flat side.

Practice producing and hiding the coin until you can do both with ease. Do not attempt the routine until you are comfortable with the handling.

The Miser's Dream

A one-pound coffee can will make a good coin pail for this routine. Remove the label and recover the can with a colorful self-adhesive contact paper. To prepare for the trick you will need five coins and a wand or long pencil. Use quarters or half-dollars for better visibility and handling. Half-dollars are best if you can handle them.

Lay the can on its side on your table so that the bottom faces the audience. Prepare only four coins by placing them into the mouth of the can, overlapping one another. The first coin is placed about two inches into the can. The next one overlaps the first one, coming closer to the rim. Each coin overlaps until all four coins rest inside the can (Fig. 41). The fifth coin is on the table next to your wand, where you can find it easily.

Carefully lift the can with your left hand. Four fingers of the left hand go inside the can so that they will cover the overlapped coins, pressing them firmly against the inside wall. The left thumb is outside the can. Pick up the wand with the other hand and tap the bottom of the can. Turn the can, allowing the audience to see inside, but do not announce that you are showing it empty. "*A solid can.*" Put the wand back on your table and secretly pick up the coin, bringing it into Down's palm position.

"*For centuries every magician has been asked this one burning question: Can you make money with magic? I will*

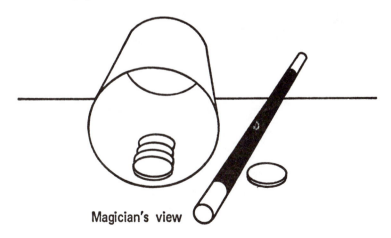

Magician's view

Fig. 41

answer the question with a simple demonstration. May I have some music, please."

If you have someone to play a piano, it is much nicer. If not, you can have a tape recorder playing some soft, soothing music in the background as you begin your demonstration.

Reach into the air and pluck the first coin by bringing it to your fingertips. As you pretend to drop it into the can, the coin goes back into its hiding place (palm position). The left hand simultaneously releases only the bottom coin of the four. The audience will hear a coin drop and will assume it is the same one you just produced.

Point to another spot in the air and produce the palmed coin again. Repeat the action of bringing the coin back to palm position and releasing the second coin from the left hand. Timing is very important here. Do not drop the coin before you make the motion of throwing it into the can.

Repeat the action two more times until four coins are in the can. Jingle them a bit so the audience hears the sound.

Here is a most deceptive move. Produce the next coin. Pretend to throw it into the can again. This time when the coin goes back to palm position strike the outer edge of the can with the base of your right pinky. If the four right fingers are held together, you will get a better sound. The impact on the rim will cause one of the coins inside to bounce. It will sound like another coin falling into the can.

Repeat this action twice more. You have apparently produced seven coins thus far. Produce the last coin but do not palm it. Toss it into the air, catching it in the can.

"And that's how a magician makes money!"

PRESTO-CHANGE!

Another waie to deceive the lookers on, is to doo as before, with testor; and keeping the counter in the palme of the left hand secretlie to seem to put the testor thereinto; which being reteined still in the right hand, when the left hand is opened, the testor will seeme to be transubstantiated into a counter.

Reginald Scot, DISCOVERIE OF WITCHCRAFT, 1584
Book XIII, Chapter XXIV

CHANGING ONE OBJECT INTO ANOTHER

The lovely lady has just stepped into a large cage, which is then covered with a sheet. In an instant the magician pulls away the cloth. In her place we see a large Bengal tiger. It is a startling trick and one that brings surprise and a great deal of applause.

Another magician can take a small red handkerchief, push it through his bare hand, and amazingly change it into a blue handkerchief.

The first example is called a "transformation." The lady has apparently been transformed into the animal. The second, simpler effect is called a "color-change." But both are transformations since one object is changed into another.

To accomplish a transformation magicians use two of their skills. They must have the ability to make things vanish and the ability to produce objects. By combining the two they create the "transformation." The lady vanishes and the tiger appears. A red scarf disappears and a blue one is produced.

When a magician substitutes one thing for another to accomplish the "transformation," it is called a "switch." In this chapter we will cover some of the methods used for this kind of illusion.

COLOR-CHANGING WAND

If you already have a wand, it probably has white plastic tips on each end of a shiny black rod. More expensive wands might have chrome tips on black metal surfaces. Wands of ancient times were ornate and hand-painted with symbols and strange characters on their surfaces. The wand is used almost entirely for misdirection. It serves as a tool to create magic for the spectator while it offers the magician opportunities to "steal," or get rid of small objects. It gives a pretext for movements that otherwise would not seem natural. The touch of the wand allows the magic to happen for the onlooker. If you haven't got a wand, here's how to make one.

Buy a 12-inch length of dowel at a lumber yard. Sand it so that it is smooth and paint all but about an inch at each end with a bright-colored paint. Let's assume you use red paint. When the wand is dry, paint one inch of white on each tip. A glossy enamel will cover any red edges still showing. When this is dry, you will have a fine-looking red wand that can be used for all your tricks.

For the color-changing effect we will also need a "feke." This is a magician's term for something that the audience can see but does not know is being used as a gimmick of a sort. In this case the "feke" is a tube or "shell" made from a piece of construction paper.

If your wand is 12 inches long with a one-inch tip on either end, the colored section measures 10 inches. Cut a 10-inch piece of construction paper of a contrasting color. For this effect we'll use green. The width of the paper should be great enough to wrap around the wand. Wrap it once around the wand and seal the loose edge with rubber cement or clear cellophane tape. The tube should be tight enough to stay on the wand. It should also be able to slide off if you pull it, so do not wrap it too tightly. It should look like a normal green wand.

Have the wand and its shell prepared on the table. You might use it for other tricks during your performance.

"By the way, how do you like my wand? I got it for Christmas."

Pick up a single sheet of tabloid-sized newspaper.

"It was wrapped just like this under the tree."

Wrap the wand by rolling the paper around it. Do not make the roll too tight. Reach into one side of the roll and pull out about two inches of the wand and tip so the audience gets a last look at the green wand. Push it back out of sight.

"I never had a green wand before. But at Christmastime most things are green. What I really wanted was a black wand. So on Christmas morning I waved my hand over the paper and it was black. . . ."

Pull the wand out so that only the white tip shows. Hold back the shell, keeping it inside the paper. Leave the white tip sticking out.

"My hand was black. . . from the newspaper. At Christmastime things are always green. . . or red."

Pull the tip completely out of the paper, leaving the shell behind. The wand will have changed to red. Crumple the newspaper and toss it away behind you.

If you are using a black wand, cover it with red or colored paper and perform the trick the same way, except change the patter to fit the colors.

CHANGING SILKS

Today's magicians call Robert-Houdin the "father of modern magic." Robert-Houdin was a French magician who lived in the mid-1800s. He was one of the first performers to use silk pocket handkerchiefs in his act. He mopped his brow and the silk vanished, being secretly pulled up into his sleeve by a cord. Before that time the handkerchiefs used by the magician were made of other bulky materials. At about the same time Buatier de Kolta discovered that silk could be compressed into small areas and would expand again when produced. Silk handkerchiefs could also be made available in a variety of bright colors and offered a great many possibilities for developing new tricks. His first "pull" vanisher was made to accommodate a silk handkerchief. Since that time magicians have been using "silks" for productions, vanishes, and color changes. There are whole books entirely devoted to silk magic.

A color change can be effected by using a "switch" whereby you secretly exchange one colored object for another. You will need two silk handkerchiefs of contrasting colors. Both must be of the same size. We will use red and yellow for the description. Magician's silk scarves are sold in squares measuring 12, 18, 24, and 36 inches.

Place a 12- or 18-inch red silk in the front section of your paper bag vanisher. The pocket remains empty. Fold the paper bag so that it will lie flat on your table. Silk does not bulk up, as you will see. Prepare the yellow silk nearby. This is how to present the effect. Pick up the yellow scarf and show it to the audience.

"We will need a red handkerchief for this next miracle."

Someone will comment that the scarf is not red. If they do not, pretend to have heard someone speaking.

"What's that? Yellow. I see red every time I make a mistake. But fear not . . . all can be saved."

The other hand picks up the paper bag. Hold one side of the bag and give it a good shake, so that the air rushes in to open the bag. Do not show the inside of the bag. Since it was flat on your table, the audience will assume it to be empty.

Poke the yellow silk into the pocket section of the vanisher.

"We'll need a few words that mean magic. . . .The check is in the mail."

Reach into the bag again, slowly pull up the red handkerchief, and drape it over the left arm with a flourish. Tear the bag apart by pulling the front panel away from your body. It is apparently empty. Crumple the bag and toss it onto the table where you can find it again after your show.

"A red handkerchief, as I started to say before . . ."

Either use the handkerchief for another trick or poke it into your pull and make it disappear.

The color change can also be made with a Candy Bag, if you use colored ping-pong balls, or a Mirror Box for small objects. Practice this—we will use it for another miracle in the next chapter.

MAGIC WASHING MACHINE

Some years ago a man named Dr. Kayton won several magician's awards for a trick he invented called "Soft Soap." The three handkerchiefs shown were soiled with ink, lipstick, and paint. He put them into a soap powder box and shook them up a bit. When they came out, they were all quite clean and the box was empty. This effect is still a standard with many magicians. Since it is still commercially sold, we cannot describe Dr. Kayton's ingenious switching method.

With some imagination this effect can be varied by using a Mirror Box. You will also need a few 12-inch silk handkerchiefs— two blue ones and three white ones. Two of the white handkerchiefs should be stained with a few blotches of blue stamp pad ink.

Prepare your Mirror Box by dividing the load chamber into two compartments. Either use a piece of cardboard or glue a small box inside. The two sections should be clearly defined.

Load the left side of the chamber with the two spotted white handkerchiefs. Another clean white one goes on top of the spotted ones. Close the top door. Place the two blue scarves in front of the mirror in front of the box and close the door. Have the box on your table, and you are ready for the presentation.

"I just bought a handy-dandy magic washing machine from a pitchman down the street. Works without soap or water. All you need is some believing power. I'll show you how it operates."

Pick up the box and open the front door. Remove the two blue handkerchiefs. Open the top door as well and show the box empty. Do not say that it is empty, merely show it around. Close the front door.

"Two beautiful white handkerchiefs . . . unfortunately stained with blue ink. But we can clean them in an instant with some handy-dandy believin' power."

Place only one of the blue scarves into the top *right* section of the load chamber. Close the top door and shake the box back and forth a few times.

"Some magical bleach is always good. One, two, three."

Open the top door and remove the single white silk from the left-hand side of the chamber. Open the front door and show the box around as you hold up the clean white silk.

"Yes, it works every time, ladies and gentlemen. I'll do it again."

Close the front door. This time pick up the blue cloth and the white one, poking them both into the right-hand side of the chamber. Close the top door and shake the box again.

"A little more believing, and yes indeed."

Open the top door and look into the box. Pretend that something has gone wrong.

"I must remember to read the instructions next time, folks. Never do a dark wash along with a white wash. The colors might run."

Remove the two stained white silks from the left side. Open the front door so everyone can see the empty box. Close the doors and put the box aside. Hold up the two stained silks.

"I think I'll use soap powder next time."

If you have a handkerchief pull vanisher ready, you could poke both silks into your hand and end with a vanish, saying . . .

"Last time I did it, it was worse. I used too much bleach and the colors were gone."

Open the hand to show it empty.

This is a very entertaining routine and is especially good for children's audiences, who love stories with their magic. You could also adapt your paper bag vanisher or partition a cardboard soap powder box for this routine. Remember that when doing it, you can only show the box empty at the end. This is why the Mirror Box is preferred, if you have one. It can be shown empty each time.

FLAG TRANSFORMATION

Production and vanishing equipment is very practical for various kinds of magic. With a bit of ingenuity you can make up your own magic tricks using standard equipment. If you combine a production and a vanish, you can perform an effect known as Blendo. This is the commercial name for the instant change of three or four medium-sized silks into a single giant scarf of the same colors. In the commercial version the cloth is gimmicked. Our simpler version uses a Paper Bag Vanisher.

Prepare a flag in the front compartment of the vanisher. Use three smaller silks of red, white, and blue. Poke the silks into the load chamber, tear the bag open, and produce the flag to end your act. It is a strong effect.

In years past many vaudeville performers would close their acts by displaying a flag. If their acts didn't get it, the flag was sure to bring applause.

MONEY – MONEY – MONEY

The transformation of one-dollar bills into five-dollar bills is an impressive closeup effect. It was taught to me by Larry Arcuri, one of New York's well-known magicians. If you visit the magician's round table at the Scandia Restaurant in New York, you can bet that Larry will be there to show this to you.

You will need five one-dollar bills and five five-dollar bills. It will be well worth the thirty dollars to make up a set.

Use rubber cement to make up a "fake" for this trick. Fold

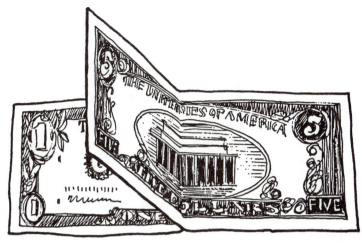

Lincoln and Washington glued face to face

Fig. 42

one of the singles in half so that when you open it again, you will
have a crease running vertically through Washington's photo.
Apply rubber cement to the right side of the bill from the crease
to the right edge of the bill (Fig. 42). Glue a five-dollar bill to the
single so that Lincoln and Washington are face to face. The green
side of the "five" will show on one side of the "fake," the green side
of the "one" will be showing on the other side. It should take only a
few minutes to dry. And if you ever need to use the money, you
can peel them apart, without damage to either bill. The rubber
cement does not produce a permanent bond.

Place this fake flat on the table so that the five-dollar side is
up. Fold the other four five-dollar bills in half, so that the picture
sides are up. The crease goes through Lincoln's portrait. Place
these bills on top of the glued half of the "fake." Fold the unglued
half of the five down to cover them. You should now see half a
one on top and half a five on the bottom.

Turn the entire pack over across your left palm. The green
side of the one-dollar bill is up. Your thumb holds all the loose
bills in place against your palm. Place three more single dollars on
top of the stack, green sides up. Place the last dollar *under* the
pile. Fold the loose halves of the bills in half toward your palm.
You can now hold the entire package under your left thumb. Mark
the top bill with a pencil dot so you can recognize it.

Here is the presentation and handling.

"I had a crazy dream last night. I was in Las Vegas and I won

twenty-five dollars in roulette. They gave me five bills. But they were all singles. . . ."

Hold the pack in the left hand with the thumb on top. The pencil dot will tell you if the right end is showing. With the right thumb you will count the bills one at a time, peeling them back into open position. Count them aloud as you open the package.

"One—two—three—four—five."

Do not remove the bills from the hand. You are going to count them again slowly, taking one bill at a time with your right hand. Place each bill under the next one as you count them. Use your left thumb to push them off carefully.

"One—two—three. . ."

At the count of *"four"* take all the bills and the fake together as one. Turn the last bill over once or twice, allowing the spectator to see both sides. Place it on *top* of the stack in the right hand.

Square all the bills and transfer them back into the left hand again. The hidden package is now back in the left palm. Fold the loose bills in half toward your body. Hold the package with the left thumb and turn your hand over so that only the back is showing.

"Dreams are crazy. But when I woke up I found the strangest thing. I had twenty-five dollars. . . ."

Pull the packet out of the left hand with the right thumb and middle finger. Place the whole package back into the left palm. The folded five is now showing. Peel the bills back as you count them one at a time, opening each bill.

"Five—ten—fifteen—twenty—twenty-five."

Hold the pack carefully so as not to expose the extra bills. Pick up the top bill and turn it over, showing both sides. Replace it *under* the bills in the left hand.

Turn the entire package over, end over end, bring the "fake" into your palm again. The picture side is in your open palm. Hold up all the bills so the audience can see their backs as you spread them apart. Make sure that the second bill is facing you and cannot be seen by anyone at your side. Put the bills in your pocket.

"Aren't dreams wonderful sometimes?"

SILK TO EGG

Another good method of creating a transformation is to hide one object inside the other. Remember the glass hidden inside the baking soda can? If the can were removed under the cover of a larger tube or an opaque cloth, the glass would remain. This would effect the change of the can into the glass.

The silk-to-egg trick is a perfect example of a transformation. It is quite inexpensive to buy and a problem to make. The egg is usually a plastic one that is hollow. It has a small hole on one side about the size of a quarter. If you make one with a real egg, take extreme care not to crack the delicate egg surface as you make the hole.

The fake egg is hidden in the palm of the left hand and held in place with the middle finger. A 12-inch silk handkerchief is waved about for a few moments and then apparently placed into the left fist. It is actually being tucked into the hole in the hollow egg. Open the hand and the egg appears. The thumb covers the hole.

By switching the fake egg for a real one, the magician can create a better illusion. Another name for this trick is the Sucker Egg trick. When sold commercially, it is usually supplied with a silk handkerchief and instructions for switching to a real egg.

COLOR-CHANGING KNIFE

One of the standard sleights a magician is required to learn is the Paddle Move. This is a method of seeming to show both sides of a flat object, but actually showing one side twice and keeping the other side hidden. It is usually done with a small paddle. I described it for use with a dinner knife in *Magic with Everyday Objects*. Here it is again, using a pocketknife.

You will need two identical pocketknives. White-handled ones are suggested, although any color can be used. The blades will remain folded inside and should not be used. Use an acrylic paint or colored nail polish to paint over one white side on one of the knives. We'll assume you are using red paint. When this is dry, you will have a knife with one color on each side. The unpainted knife remains in your pocket until after the trick is over. These knives are commercially available should you decide not to make your own.

1. This is the basic move. Hold the knife across the right fingers, white side showing. The blade edge is facing your fingertips. Your right thumb is on top of the knife. The knife should rest on the second joint of your middle finger, as in Figs. 43 and 44.

    Push the knife toward your fingertips with your thumb so that it rolls over and shows the red side. Roll it to the white side by pulling it back with your thumb. This is called the "half" turn. Practice this a few times, until it is easy to maneuver.

2. Hold the knife in your hand at about waist level in front of you. The white side is showing. Turn your right wrist in toward your body, giving the knife a half turn at the same time. The knife turns toward your chin as you

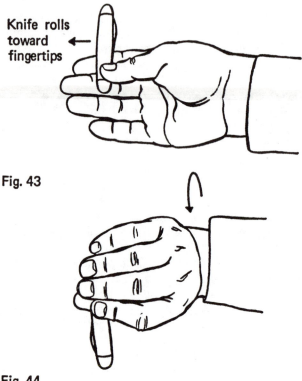

Knife rolls
toward ←
fingertips

Fig. 43

Fig. 44

move the wrist. You will see the same white side again. You have apparently shown both sides of the knife, but in fact have only shown one side twice. This position is called the "up" position. Reverse the moves and bring the knife back to its original position. Practice this a few times.

3. Bring the knife to "up" position. Your palm should be facing the floor. You will now change the color of the knife by turning your wrist back to its original position *without* turning the knife at all. Bring the wrist down with a snapping movement to call attention to motion.

4. Repeat the original steps 1 and 2 with the red side of the knife. Show it red on both sides.

You have just learned a classic closeup trick that should be practiced for smooth natural movement. Do not be in a hurry to show the sides of the knife. The moves should be slow and deliberate.

Here is a routine for the color-changing knife. Keep the extra knife in your pocket, separated from the fake knife so you can tell them apart. Remove the fake knife so that the white side is showing as you begin the patter.

"I must show you this terrific birthday present I got from a friend of mine. Isn't it beautiful? And the white matches my teeth."

Turn the knife over a few times to show the white color. Bring the knife to "up" position.

"I have a new red sport jacket I bought last week. I'll bet a red knife would look great with that jacket."

Change the color of the knife to red. Turn it over a few times to establish that it has changed color. Bring it back to "up" position.

"It's too bad I don't have a red knife."

Change the color to white again and turn it a few more times.

"But I guess white is a color that goes with any suit."

Put the knife into your pocket and exchange it for the real unfaked one. Bring it out immediately as though you forgot to show something else.

"Here. Would you like to take a look at it? Check the blade and see how sharp it is."

Hand the knife to your spectator, who can examine it all he likes. It is a real knife and ungimmicked.

There are many variations of the paddle trick and the color-changing knife trick. Once you have mastered the moves, you can expand your knowledge with other techniques.

TRANSPOSITIONS

CHANGING PLACES

The pretty young lady is securely tied into a bag and locked inside a heavy packing case. The magician seals the entire case inside a heavy canvas bag and then chains the sides and top, locking them together with sturdy padlocks. Two spectators assist with the tying process. The magician now climbs on top of the case, holding a large cloth in front of his body. In an instant the cloth drops and the magician is gone. In his place stands the lovely young lady we saw earlier. She and the spectators unlock the padlocks and remove the chains and canvas from around the box. The box is opened, and the top of the sack is untied. There stands the magician, hands in handcuffs, smoking a cigarette. This presentation is currently being performed by Denny and Lee.

At one time or another you must have seen a variation of this trick on TV or in a theater. Doug Henning performs this inside of a trunk, coming out with a change of costume. The trick was popularized by Harry Houdini under the name of "Metamorphosis." The title suggests a physical change, but this is not quite accurate.

When two things are made to change places with one another, we call it a transposition. If we analyze the effect again, we see that we are using two transformations accomplished by a switch. Let's study a few of the transpositions that we perform.

FLYING ROPE

The Passe-Passe bottle trick is a classic transposition in the world of magic. A cylinder covers a bottle on one side of the stage. Another cylinder covers a glass on the opposite end. The glass and bottle change places several times at the command of the magician.

One object must hide inside the other. The baking soda can prop we described earlier hides a glass inside. If two sets are made this way, it will allow you to lift a can and produce a glass or to cover a glass and reveal a can. The cylinders that hide the action must have holes in the back to enable you to control the lifting. This effect is sold commercially under various names—Soda-Chaser, Can and Glass Transpo, Passe-Passe Soda, etc.

The same effect of Passe-Passe can be done with other types of props using the Vanish and Production props. Here is how it can be done with a rope.

Prepare two Paper Bag Vanishers. A number-6 grocery bag is a handy size to use. One bag will be used as a vanisher, the other for a production. By alternating the use of the bags we will create our transposition.

Cut two four-foot lengths of soft rope. If you remove the inside batting, the ropes will be softer and easier to handle. Tie a knot in the exact center of one of the pieces and place the rope inside the load chamber of one of the bags. We'll call this bag #1. Put the second length of rope in the front section of the same bag. Lay the bag on your table so that the audience cannot see inside. The opening should face the rear of the table. The second bag (#2) should be flat on the table to the left of the first bag. Stand behind your table as you present the effect.

"I have often heard about flying carpets being used in Persia. The magician sat up front in first class with his assistant behind him in the tourist section. They flew from place to place. I made a Persian-to-Persian phone call and asked my Dad to send me a piece of rope. It is the same kind of rope used for making flying carpets. I have it here."

Pick up bag #1 and remove the single length of rope from the front of the bag. Drape the rope over your arm as you show the bag empty by pressing the middle wall against the rear section. Set the bag on your table so that it will stand up at your right.

"This rope came from Baghdad in that bag. It was the only bag Dad had."

Lift bag #2, open it, and show it empty, as you did before. Set this on the table so that it stands at your left.

> *"The rope itself has the power to fly. Watch how I make it fly from this bag to that!"*

Drop the exposed rope into bag #2. Make a magical gesture with your wand, pointing it from bag #2 to bag #1.

> *"The rope has flown from the empty bag on my left to the empty bag on my right. This filled up the second bag leaving the first bag empty again. Did you follow that? No? I'll do it again. This time, please pay attention."*

Make another pass, gesturing from bag #1 to bag #2.

> *"It is done. The rope is now back in the original bag, having flown nonstop."*

Slowly lift the rope out of bag #2.

> *"I know what you are thinking. You are thinking that this is not the same piece of rope. Let me mark it this time."*

Tie a knot in the exact center of the rope. It must match the one that is still in the load chamber of bag #1. Open bag #2 and lower the knotted rope into the load chamber.

> *"The rope flies again from this bag to that."*

After another gesture with your wand, reach into bag #1 and draw the rope from the load chamber. Show the bag empty. Now pick up bag #2 and tear the front section away from the bag to show it empty. The rope is still hidden in the back load area. Crumple the paper bag and toss it aside casually.

> *"If I could only get more of this rope, I could make a DC-10 and fly first class."*

This effect can be a nice transition if you decide to do a rope trick. Using the same rope for another trick blends the two together and logically routines your magic act.

RIBBON OF THE ORIENT

This is another Passe-Passe effect done a different way. We will use liquid and a surprise ending.

You will need four paper cups—two large opaque cups and two much smaller ones. The small ones should be about the size used in bathroom drinking cup dispensers. You will also need a glass or pitcher of clear water, a few drops of vegetable food coloring, and two lengths of ribbon, each about a yard long. The ribbons should be the same color as the coloring you will use (green, yellow, red, or blue).

Carefully remove the top outer lip of the two smallest cups so that they have no raised rims. Staple the smaller cups inside the larger ones, close to the top. A single staple is enough to secure them. This gives you two gimmicked or prepared cups. A gimmick is something used to accomplish a trick that the audience never sees. Make sure they will never see the inside of these cups.

Designate one cup as A and one cup as B. One length of ribbon is tucked into the larger cup section of cup A. Allow the last half-inch to stick up just inside the lip of the cup, so you can pull it out easily when needed. Fill the inner cup with clear water, a bit more than half full. Cup A is set on your table, mouth up.

Prepare cup B with the other length of ribbon in the outer cup area. Then tuck it under the small cup so it will not fall out. Now drop three or four drops of food coloring into the inner B cup. Shake it up a bit so that the coloring covers the bottom of the inner cup. Invert the cup over a small piece of newspaper on your table next to cup A. The newspaper will serve to absorb any droplets of dye that are still loose. The glass of water or clear pitcher is at the right (Fig. 45). Present the effect as follows:

"The great Chinese philosopher Confucius once said..." (Pause to think for a few moments) *"Many things.... Oh yes, he said 'A man who keeps a long ribbon in his cup... had better be a magician, or he will look pretty silly.'"*

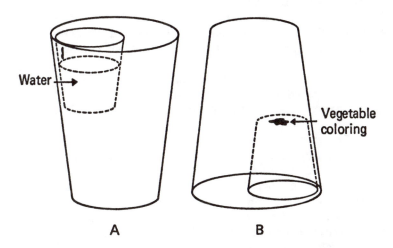

Water

Vegetable coloring

A   B

Fig. 45

Casually lift cup A and remove the ribbon with a flourish. Set the glass down again, being careful not to spill the liquid inside. Display the ribbon.

"This is known as the ribbon of the Orient."

Slowly push the ribbon back into the front of the cup as you continue.

"It is a mysterious ribbon that moves about from place to place, changing its form to become invisible at times."

As you speak, lift up cup B, taking care not to expose the mouth of the cup. Lift the pitcher and slowly pour some water into the inner cup, filling it only half full. Set the cup on the table.

"It can become as clear as this water. Watch the ribbon rise from the cup."

A little acting here can't hurt. Pretend to see the ribbon rising from cup A and moving about in the air in front of you.

"Can you see it suspended right here? It is almost invisible to the untrained eye."

Look at someone in the audience.

"You see it, sir? I think you're in trouble. Watch the ribbon pass from the air into this cup of water."

Lift cup B and gently remove the ribbon from the inside. Hold it up for all to see as you set the cup on the table again.

"It is completely dry, ladies and gentlemen. There is a reason for this. The water is from the Ganges River. It changes to vapor and travels the Orient through the atmosphere, passing into the other cup."

Drape the ribbon over your shoulder as you lift cup A. Poor the water out of the smaller cup and into the pitcher. Keep the mouth of the cup facing away from the audience. Set the cup on the table again.

"One of the most curious things is that science has not been able to explain this phenomenon."

As you speak, push the ribbon carefully into the front section of cup B.

"The water could possibly evaporate."

Pour water from the pitcher into the inner section of cup A. Wave the hand, making a magical pass from cup to cup.

"The ribbon might pass unseen through mass hypnosis."

Pull the ribbon from cup A and show it again.

"But what science and Confucius cannot explain is this . . ."

Pour the colored water from cup B into the pitcher.

"Which I prefer to explain simply as magic!"

THE DEVIL LOSES

When we speak of illusions, we picture large boxes and heavy pieces of magical equipment. Here is a stage illusion that requires very little and is highly entertaining. It is one that can be made inexpensively. This transposition will involve a few children.

You will need three costumes for this effect—two identical, brightly colored Princess costumes and a third costume of black or deep red, to represent a Devil. Each costume will be made to fit over the children's clothing. All the costumes are in two pieces. One section is a robelike piece of cloth with a hole at the top for

Loose robe costume and hooded mask hide child. Note star on a dowel to serve as scepter.

Fig. 46

the child's head. The cloth covers the entire child from the neck down to the floor, hiding hands and feet. The second part of the costume is a hooded mask that fits over the child's head so you cannot tell if there is a boy or girl under the robe. Two of the masks will depict the Princess; the other one bears the face of the Devil. I always use an ugly old lady mask, whom I call a "pretty Princess" for comedy. Make sure that all the masks have eyeholes and plenty of breathing room inside.

The Princess will also need one scepter, which can be made of a three-foot dowel topped with a Christmas star ornament. The scepter and one of the Princess costumes remain backstage with someone who will act as your assistant. This person should not be seen during the performance. If there is no backstage area, you can use a large screen to hide the assistant.

The other two costumes are conveniently placed on a chair onstage to the right of the magician. Have the masks folded inside the costumes so they will not be seen until later. Follow these 10 steps carefully so that you have a complete understanding of the mechanics and staging of this illusion. (Fig. 46.)

1. You will need three children—a boy and two girls—all of about the same height. You must be careful when inviting children onstage. Never ask for volunteers outright, or the stage will be mobbed with running, noisy children. Phrase the invitation with care.

    "Will a few boys and girls who would like to help me please stand up at your seats."

    While the children are standing, you can estimate their heights and you can easily select three children of about the same size. The length of the costumes will determine the maximum limits of size. Invite the children onstage and introduce them to one another. Have them shake hands, offer their names, and place them in position for the trick.

2. The boy is positioned to your immediate left. Designate one of the girls to play the part of the Princess, having her to the boy's left. The other girl is at the far left. She will assist as your *"Wardrobe Lady, who will help us with the costumes."*

3. Give the Princess costume and its hidden mask to the Wardrobe Lady. Instruct the two girls.

    "If you lovely ladies will go backstage, the Princess can get into her costume for this demonstration.

> *Our Wardrobe Lady will help her with the costume.*"

Send both girls backstage.

4. A. Backstage, your assistant dresses the child who is carrying the costume—that is, the Wardrobe Lady. The Princess costume and the hood will completely cover the girl so that no one can tell who is under the hood. When the child is dressed, the assistant sends her onstage, keeping the "real" Princess backstage.

B. On the stage, meantime, the magician is still with the boy. During the time of the costume change the magician explains the story the children will act out.

> *"There was an old legend told by the Indians in South America, about a trick they once played on the wicked Devil. The chieftain had given his Indian Princess a scepter that had special powers to help her do good things for their people. She was a beautiful princess. Here she comes now."*

Speak slowly enough to allow for the timing of the last line to coincide with the girl's entrance. The Wardrobe Girl comes out dressed as the Princess. If you are using an ugly old lady mask it is more comical since you just described the Princess as "pretty."

5. Hand the Devil costume to the boy and have him go back to get dressed.

> *"You will play an important part in this story, so please get into costume and come right back. The Wardrobe Lady will help you with your costume."*

6. A. Backstage, your assistant takes the costume the boy is carrying. She dresses the *girl* in the Devil outfit and keeps the *boy* backstage. The girls is sent out front. As soon as the girl goes out, the assistant dresses the boy in the extra Princess costume. He is given the scepter to hold through the cloth in the costume.

B. On the stage, to give them time for the second change, you will repeat the story you told the audience for the benefit of the girl on the stage. You will finish the story with

> *"You will play the part of the Princess. And here comes the Devil now."*

Position the Devil to your right so that you are in between the two children. Both girls are on the stage, unknown to the audience.

7.   *"The Devil was mean, and he wanted to destroy the village and burn it to the ground. But he couldn't do it as long as the Princess had the magic scepter."*

Point to the Princess.

"Where is the scepter? Please run backstage and get it for us. Thanks."

Send the Princess (actually the Wardrobe Girl) back to get the scepter.

8. A.   Backstage, your assistant keeps the girl and sends out the boy. He is dressed as the Princess and is carrying the scepter. Once the boy is out front, the assistant removes the costume from the Wardrobe Girl.

   B.   On the stage, you acknowledge the return of the Princess.

"Good. There is the magic scepter."

Look around you for a moment, then interrupt the story.

"Where is the Wardrobe Girl? (Beckon backstage.) Come on out, I don't want you to miss the fun. Let's all give her a nice round of applause for helping us. Sit out in front so you can watch the play."

Have the child seated while you continue your story.

9.   *"The Devil had to have the magic scepter out of the way in order for him to do his dirty work. He tried to steal it, but couldn't."* (Adlib: *"He couldn't get his hands out of his costume."*) *"The Princess warned him, 'If you try to steal the star, I'll turn you into a pretty person and you'll never be able to frighten anyone again.' And that's what she did."*

Point to the child with the scepter.

"Wave the wand please. You did it! The old devil became a beautiful person."

Remove the hooded mask from the Devil to reveal the girl.

10. Take the scepter from the other child and wave it over his head.

"And as for the Princess, she turned out to be a handsome Devil after all."

Pull the hood off to reveal the boy.

The presentation and timing are very important to this effect. Backstage, your assistant must tell the children what parts they will play and not to speak. For example, she will tell the Wardrobe Girl, *"You'll be the Princess for a little while."* She tells the second girl, *"You will pretend to be the Devil."* She instructs the boy that he is going to *"fool everyone and pretend to be the Princess."* In this way the children will not be tempted to shout out their comments about being in the wrong costumes.

With some ingenuity you can change the story to fit any characters. You can change masks to accommodate your story, too. For a church play you can have the Princess character as an Angel. You can portray the children as Space People or Astronauts, and so on. The illusion is sold commercially and is available with the masks and costumes as the *"Farmer and the Witch,"* from Abbott's Magic Company in Colon, Michigan.

RESTORATIONS

To cut a lace asunder in the middest, and to make it whole againe. . .

**Reginald Scot, DISCOVERIE OF WITCHCRAFT, 1584
Book XIII, Chapter XXXII**

BACK TO NORMAL

Khufu was a king of ancient Egypt who lived about 2600 B. C. The Greeks called him King Cheops. Historians remember him for his tomb, the Great Pyramid at Gizeh, one of the seven wonders of the ancient world. Magic buffs remember him for his magician, Dedi. Dedi did an impossible trick which was described in a document called the Westcar papyrus written in 1700 B. C., before the time of Moses.

It is said that Dedi cut off the head of a goose. When the head and body were put together again, the goose ran off, restored to life.

The Sawing a Lady in Half illusion performed by Goldin in 1921 was a version of the same trick done 4,000 years earlier. An object, having been destroyed, is magically restored to its original form. This is known in magic as a Restoration.

CUTTING AND RESTORING A ROPE
Classic Method

Most modern-day magicians perform one or another of the many variations of the restoration effect. The most popular form of this trick is the classic Cut and Restored Rope Trick. Early magicians did it with string as a pocket trick. It was Dr. Harlan Tarbell who substituted rope for string and opened the door for its use on the stage.

The effect is simply this. A length of rope is cut in half. The two pieces are knotted together and in a flash the magician restores the rope to a single length again.

If you use a cloth bag or other vanisher prop, you can switch the pieces, substituting them for a whole piece. This method is used for the Cut and Restored Necktie trick most often. But it is much more effective if you do the trick visibly, while the rope is in full view.

The most effective way to perform the trick is by a classic method enabling you to make it appear that the rope is cut in half, when in fact it is not. Since no one actually measures the rope before you start, you can simulate the effect by cutting off only a small piece.

The rope that magicians use is soft braided cotton clothesline. The difference between this and a regular clothesline is that it is unglazed and does not have the stiff outer finish. Soft rope is best purchased in the magic shops. You might also try soft venetian blind cord. If you use a regular clothesline, I suggest you boil it in a pot of water so as to remove the chemical glaze. This will make it soft again. Hang it out to dry so that it does not curl.

You will need a four-foot length of rope and a pair of sharp scissors. Have the scissors in your right-hand coat pocket and follow these 10 steps:

1. Hold the rope in the left hand between the thumb and forefinger, about an inch from the top. The little finger is clipped over the rope as shown in Fig. 47.

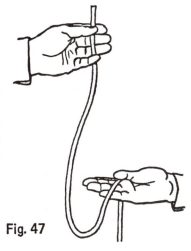

Fig. 47

2. Lift the rope with the right hand just above the center of the rope so that it lies across the middle joints of the outstretched fingers. The right hand is turned so that the palm is facing up.

3. Now turn the right hand in toward your body. The center of the rope will be lying across the back of the right fingers. Move the right hand up and clip the rope about an inch below the left little finger. Fig. 48 shows how the hands should look. Note that the right-index and middle fingers are used to clip the rope. The left little finger releases its hold at this point (Fig. 48).

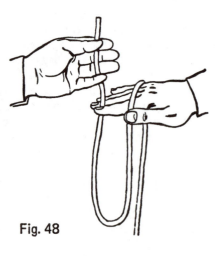

Fig. 48

4. Raise your right hand so that it comes up higher than the left hand. As you do this, the rope will slide off the back of the right hand. This forms a small loop, which you can hold with the left thumb (Figs. 49, 50.)

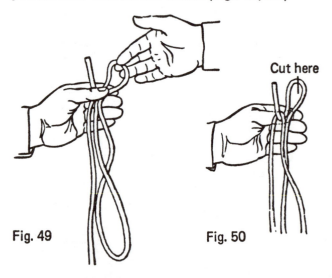

Cut here

Fig. 49   Fig. 50

5. With the left hand holding all the rope, the right hand is free to go to the pocket and remove the scissors. Cut the rope at the loop. (See Fig. 49.) After the cut, put the scissors back in your pocket. The audience sees two lengths of rope as shown in Fig. 51. In reality there is a single rope, doubled in half, with a small extra piece of rope around it. Your thumb will hide the separation. Fig. 52 shows you what you would see if the thumb were removed.

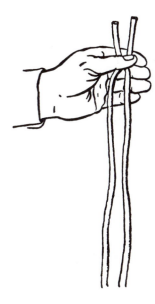

Fig. 51

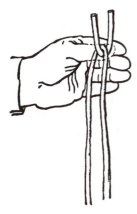

Fig. 52

6.   *"Two pieces with four ends. One on each."*
        Tie a simple knot in the small rope joining ends A and B
        (Fig. 51). Take the scissors out of your pocket again and
        trim off the ends of the knot.

7.   Pick up end C or D with the left hand. The audience
     sees a single length of rope with a knot in the center.
     They believe they are seeing two pieces joined together.
     Clip the top of the rope between the thumb and index
     fingers of the left hand. The rope should hang over the
     back of the left hand.

8.   With the right hand, which is still holding the scissors,
     begin to wrap the rope around the left fingers. The
     wrapping is done in a motion rotating in the direction
     away from your body.

9.   As you wrap the rope, you will come to the knot, which
     will slide along inside your right fingers and come off
     the end of the rope. The extra knot will be hidden by
     your right hand. Put the scissors back in your right coat
     pocket along with the extra piece of the knot.

10. Unwind the rope again and show it to be a single res-
     tored length. Practice the cutting and knotting effect in
     front of a mirror so you can see what the audience sees.

Square Knot, Please

You can either tie this one yourself or you can allow a spectator
to help you. Ask someone if he or she knows how to tie a square
knot. This is a knot tied by bringing the right end of your rope
over the left, then the left over the right. Use a four-foot length of
rope.

Hand the rope to your spectator.

*"I am going to cut this rope into two equal pieces. I need a
square knot in the middle of the rope. Please tie this knot for
me, bringing one of the ends up to the center."*

Allow the spectator to do this, but watch to make sure that a square knot is being tied. No other knot will work. If the knot is being tied incorrectly, stop the action.

"Only a square knot, please."

Once the rope has been tied, thank your spectator and take back the rope, holding it in your left hand through the loop. The extra length of rope should be hanging downward at the *right* side of the loop (your view).

Using a sharp scissors, cut the rope inside the loop about one-half inch above the knot (Fig. 53). Snip off the surplus ends of the knot, being careful not to cut the knot itself. It is very delicate at this point. Hold the rope horizontally, one end in each hand.

"Two pieces of rope held with a knot. First it is . . ."

Snap the rope, pulling it taut. The false knot will fly off into the air, and the rope is seen restored.

". . . and now it's not!"

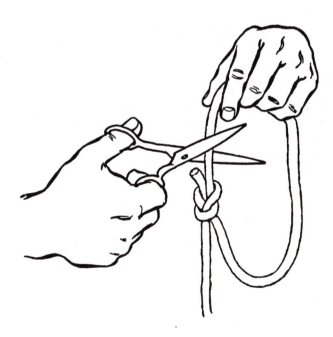

Fig. 53

Pull It Away

This lightning method apparently restores a cut rope to its original size. In reality the rope is never cut at all—it is all done with an extra loop. This may be very sneaky, but it is quite effective on any stage.

Prepare a short piece of rope about five inches in length. Fold the rope in half and tie the ends with a strong thread or a piece of clear fishing line. This gives you a loop of rope which you will attach to a length of elastic, making a pull. The total length of the elastic will depend upon where you are going to attach it. I suggest that you pin it inside the back of your jacket, just under the collar, so that it hangs straight down the spinal column. A three- or four-foot length of elastic will be easy to reach and gives you better mobility later.

The other piece of rope should be about five feet in length. This is prepared on your table, which should be at your left. A pair of sharp scissors is in your right coat pocket.

To present the effect, turn your whole body to your left, facing the table. Your left hand is now out of the audience's view. Secure the extra loop while the right hand picks up the other rope. Move your entire body to your right. The audience sees your left side.

Drape the rope over the back of the left hand so that its center is resting on the first joint of the left index finger (Fig. 54). The left thumb is holding the hidden loop. The elastic pull will be hidden along the left arm.

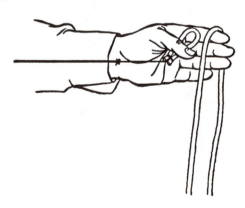

Fig. 54

Your left thumb goes into the loop. Push the loop upward, bending the left index finger into the palm. The other three fingers curl around the rope and the bottom of the loop. All this is done while the right hand goes into the pocket for the scissors.

The loose rope and the loop look like a single loop showing over the back of the left hand.

Cut the false loop. Put the scissors away in the pocket. The audience sees four ends, two on top and two hanging. Bring the hanging ends up with the right hand, placing them alongside the cut ends. The left thumb holds them all in place. Four ends are now showing in the left hand. Press the index finger and thumb together, holding one of the real ends firmly. Open the hand as you snap the rope outward in a quick gesture.

This will release the loop ends and carry them under the coat without being seen. You will be left with a single length of rope in one piece. You could do the move on the count of "three" for extra effect.

RESTORING HUMPTY DUMPTY

In this restoration we are going to use paper. The trick has many names, but it is basically a "torn and restored" effect. You can tear and restore napkins, newspapers, certificates, dollar bills, or plain pieces of paper. To make it interesting we will add a story line.

Take a few sheets of paper lighter than standard typing paper. Cut the sheets into strips about two and half inches wide by a foot long. You need two identical sheets for the trick. Print the words "HUMPTY-DUMPTY" across both sheets of paper. Make up a bunch of them at one time, and you'll have them ready when you need them.

What we are going to do is switch a group of torn pieces for a whole piece. To make the switch almost mechanical we'll employ some rubber cement or glue. Here is what you must do.

Place one of the sheets on the table, printing side down. Put a small dab of rubber cement about one inch in from the end of the strip. The dab does not cover the whole paper; it is only about an inch square.

Take another sheet and hold it face up. The printing faces you. Fold the two ends in toward the middle so that the paper is now in thirds. The printing is inside the folds. Fold that piece in thirds again the same way, so you have a small package a little over an inch in size. Glue the back of this with another dab of rubber cement. Dab the cement only in the center of the strip. Allow it to dry for a moment, then set it neatly on the first piece of paper. All the edges should line up.

Fold the top and bottom edges of the small package into an even smaller bundle, which is now glued to the original piece. This is your gimmicked strip.

You can fold the whole strip in half so that the printing is on the outside and the package is hidden inside. Glue is used so that the loose pieces will stay together later on.

Open the sheet to display the words.

"Humpty-Dumpty. Remember that story? What a waste. Humpty-Dumpty sat on a wall. Big mistake right there. He should have used a chair. So naturally Humpty-Dumpty had a great fall. Poor guy went to pieces."

Start to tear the sheet into four sections. Hold the package behind the strip with your right thumb. Tear the strip into pieces, each about the same size. Place each piece in front of the other so that all the pieces end up in front of the package. Now fold them down neatly in front of the package, making four folds in all.

Turn the package over in your hands so that it faces the audiences. The pieces are nearest you.

"All the King's horses and all the King's men couldn't put the old boy together again. Shame, too. He was a good egg. That's just a bad yolk. He should have called a magician. We could have put him together again, like this."

Open the strip by opening the folds of the package. The paper appears to be restored. The torn pieces are pasted behind the strip. Crumple the papers and toss them aside or put them into your pocket.

M' LADY'S NECKLACE

People relate best to familiar objects that they can recognize rather than unusual-looking magician's props. Nothing can be more natural than a piece of jewelry worn by someone in the audience.

Have your assistant or a friend wear a string of beads or an imitation pearl necklace. Make sure that she is sitting near the stage.

You will also need a fancy stemmed cocktail or champagne glass, a small pair of scissors, and a length of string the same size as the necklace. Roll the string into a small ball and put it next to the glass and scissors on your table.

> *"Excuse me for just a moment, but there is a lady sitting there who is wearing a most beautiful piece of jewelry that has been very distracting. Madam, I wonder if you would be so kind as to lend me your lovely necklace for a few moments so I can show it to the audience. Does it come off easily? Thank you."*

All of this is the showmanship, the build-up. You already know the lady and know that the necklace comes off. Take the necklace with your right hand. Open it so that the clasp is at the top and the beads are dangling in front of you. Walk back to the stage and hold it up for everyone to see.

> *"I wish I had a magnifying glass."*

Saying this, your left hand goes to the table. Secretly take the string between the index and middle fingers as you lift the glass by its stem with the thumb and index fingers. Look at the beads through the glass. Then set the glass back onto the table. Transfer the top of the necklace to the left hand.

> *"I once saw this test for fine pearls (or gems). You tap them with something made of metal and they make an unusual sound."*

Pick up the scissors as you speak. Tap the bottom of the necklace a few times with the point of the scissors. On the third tap make a loud snap at the bottom of the necklace. Do not cut the necklace but pretend that something has gone wrong.

> *"Oops! I didn't mean to cut it like that."*

Quickly bring the necklace over the glass. The scissors are still in your right hand. Here is the move you must learn.

Lower the left hand so that the necklace is directly over the glass. The fingers of the right hand pull up on one end of the hidden string, while the left hand simultaneously drops the beads into the glass. This should be done in one single action almost immediately after having cut at the necklace. It will appear as if the string were holding the beads together (Fig. 55).

Set the scissors aside and hold up the string. Pick up the glass and shake the beads. They will rattle in the glass as though they were loose.

> *"I really am very sorry madam. Perhaps I can fix it. Does anyone have any glue?"*

Take the end of the string in your right hand and roll it into a ball with the fingers. Pretend to take the little ball in the left hand but retain it in the right. The right hand lifts the glass by its

Fig. 55

stem as the left hand pretends to put the string into the glass.
Shake the beads again inside the glass. Walk toward the lady.
   "Take these to your jeweler and send me the bill."
On second thought, turn and walk back to your table.
   "Wait a minute. I'm supposed to be a magician."
Wave the scissors over the top of the glass. Swing the glass upward
so that the necklace flies out. Catch it with the other hand. Walk
back to the lady and return the necklace.
   "Here it is, better than new."

SOLID THROUGH SOLID

A notable feate of fast or loose; namlie, to pull three beadstones from off a cord, while you hold fast the ends thereof, without removing of your hand.

Reginald Scot, DISCOVERIE OF WITCHCRAFT, 1584
Book XIII, Chapter XXIX

PENETRATIONS

The Linking Ring illusion is one of the world's oldest magic tricks. A solid steel ring is apparently passed through another one, linking them together. They are unlinked as easily as linked when in the hands of a magician. This feat defies the laws of physics, which tell us that a solid object cannot pass through another solid object. And yet the conjuror seems to defy the laws of science with this effect. It is called the Penetration.

Using the Table Sweep you learned earlier, you can vanish a coin from the top of a table and cause it to reappear under the table. It will look as through the coin penetrated the solid tabletop. Merely sweep the coin into your lap with the right hand. Pretend to slap the coin into the center of the table with the same hand. Your left hand picks up the coin from your lap and pretends that it came through the table as you bring it up from underneath.

In *Magic with Everyday Objects* I described a Salt Shaker Vanish into the lap. This can also be presented as the penetration through a table.

Another one of the world's oldest tricks is the Cups and Balls. There are literally hundreds of variations of this trick as performed throughout history. Three little balls vanish, appear, or penetrate the solid cups at the magician's will. This is usually done with sleight of hand. The simplest version of Cups and Balls involves a penetration.

CUPS AND BALLS

The ancient Cups and Balls effect was depicted on the walls of the Beni Hasan tomb in Egypt around 2500 B.C. The sketch depicts a magician performing for his spectator. A sphere or ball was probably about to penetrate or appear under one of the four bowls seen in the picture. Hieroglyphics above the picture were translated to read, "Up from under."

For our effect we will use cups instead of bowls. Use three large paper coffee containers. (Do not use the kind with handles.) There is usually a small depression on the bottom of the cup. One cup should be able to nest inside the other one.

We will also use four cotton balls or sponges. If we were to use heavier plastic or metal cups, the balls could be made of cork or rubber. Cotton balls are fine because they will fall silently.

Prepare the cups before you start. Place one of the four balls inside one of the cups. Nest the other two cups so that the ball is hidden in the bottom of the three-cup stack. Set this on your table, mouth up, and add the other three balls, dropping them into the mouth of the top cup. You are ready to perform the trick. Now, follow these 10 steps:

1. Lift the stack of cups with your left hand and pour the three balls onto the table. Using your right hand, arrange them in a neat horizontal row across the table in front of you.

2. You will now turn the cups, mouth down, onto the table one at a time in a special manner. The right hand approaches the cups, palm up. The right index finger presses against the bottom of the stack. The right thumb and middle finger are on either side of the cup. The bottom cup is drawn downward away from the stack. The right wrist turns over (palm down) and places the cup and its ball onto the center of the table. The action is done in a single, unhurried, continuous motion that will keep the ball from being seen (Figs. 56, 57).

   The second cup is taken off the stack in the same manner and with the same unhurried motion. This is set, mouth down, to the right of the first cup. The last cup

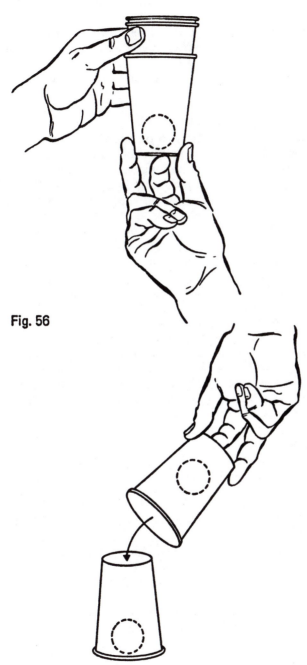

Fig. 56

Fig. 57

is taken in the right hand and set down the same way. This cup goes to the left of the other cups. The middle cup covers the hidden ball.

3. Pick up the middle ball and set it on top of the center cup.

> *"I shall attempt to make this ball penetrate the bottom of this solid cup."*

Cover the ball with the cup on the right. Cover both cups with the one on the left. They are all nested in the center of the table. Tap the topmost cup for effect.

4. All three cups will be picked up in a special way. The left hand turns over, grasping the cups between the index finger and thumb. (Fig. 58.) The wrist turns up again so that the stack is now mouth up, as if you were about to drink from the cups. (Fig. 59.) This move reveals the ball on the table which appears to have penetrated the first cup.

5. Turn the cups over again one at a time in the same fashion as in step #1. The first cup goes to your extreme right. The next one (hiding the ball) goes to the center of the table, directly covering the ball that has just penetrated. The last cup goes to the left. The middle cup is now covering two balls.

6. Pick up the second ball and set it atop the center cup. Cover this with the right-hand cup and then cover both again with the left-hand cup.

> *"We'll do it again."*

Tap the top of the stack.

7. Lift the stack as in step #4. Show the second ball to have penetrated the cup. Remove the cups from the stack again, setting the first one to your right, the middle one to cover the two balls, and the last one at your left.

8. > *"This time we'll make it harder. The ball will penetrate two of the cups."*

Pick up the last ball with the left hand. Cover the center cup with the cup on the right. Then place the ball on top of the two cups before covering the stack with the last cup. Tap the stack.

9. On lifting the stack again, three balls are revealed on the table. Remove the bottom cup and turn it down onto the table away from the other three balls. Set the other two cups down, one on each side of the middle cup. Show one of the cotton balls and bring it under the

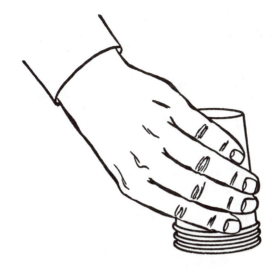

Fig. 58

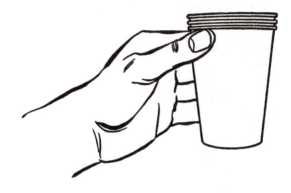

Fig. 59

table. Leave it in your lap, but reach under the table with the hand so that it is at a point directly under the center cup.

10. *"This time the ball will go through the table and under the cup."*

Tap the bottom of the table, then bring your empty hand up. Use the same hand to turn the cup over, revealing the ball. There are now three balls and three cups on the table. All can be examined by your spectators. At a convenient time later, get rid of the ball in your lap.

The routine exactly as described here is taught to our students at the School for Magicians in New York City. I want to thank the school for allowing me to use it.

PERSIAN BEGGAR'S RING TRICK

This is another classic penetration that can be accomplished by numerous methods. It is also known as the "ring on the wand." This simple impromptu method requires no sleight of hand and is most unbelievable.

Use either a wand, a very long pencil, a drumstick, or a chopstick. You will also need a gold-colored finger ring that will fit on your right little finger. You can purchase one from a dime store and carry it in your pocket.

Put the ring onto your chopstick or wand. The fingers of your right hand curled around the stick will hide the ring. You will be able to move the hand freely along the stick, and the ring will slide along with it. Be very casual as you handle the stick and do not call attention to it as yet.

"I would like to attempt an old Persian trick often performed by the beggars in the street markets of old Baghdad. For this miracle I would like to borrow a gold ring."

Accept the ring in the open palm of your left hand. Do not close the palm; let the audience see the ring in full view.

"The peddlers always carried a stick or a twig. I will use a chopstick (wand, etc.)"

Show the stick casually, holding it aloft for a moment. Then place the far end of the stick into the ring on the left palm, lifting it off the hand (Fig. 60). Hold it up gently so that everyone can see the ring sitting there. Move your right hand and its hidden ring to the center of the stick.

"The peddlers performed the miracle as follows."

Tip the wand upward so that the spectator's ring slides down toward the middle. As soon as it is covered by your fingers, relax the pressure of your hand to allow the extra ring to slide off into the waiting left hand. (Fig. 61). Your right hand is now hiding the borrowed ring on the stick.

Close the left hand. Extend the wand or stick horizontally toward the spectator.

"Please hold the ends of the stick, one in each hand."

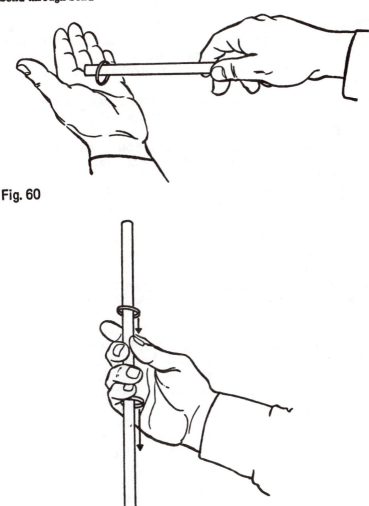

Fig. 60

Fig. 61

The left hand moves the extra ring so that the bottom of the gold band is showing at the tips of the thumb and first two fingers. The ring is not actually shown but is "flashed" for a moment. It is assumed that this is the borrowed ring.

The spectator is holding the tips of the stick. Your right hand is still in the center, covering the borrowed ring. The left hand now comes up and moves directly over and in front of the right hand. The right pinky straightens out under cover of the left hand. The extra ring is placed on the right pinky.

"The beggar would place the ring directly onto the staff. Like this!"

With one sudden gesture both hands now come away from the stick, fingers spread open and palms up. Make a strange *"Hah"* sound as you do this for extra effect. The action should be quick so that the borrowed ring is left spinning on the stick in the spectator's hands. The extra ring is never noticed since it is natural for you to be wearing one.

In the event that a gold ring is not available, do the trick anyway. The spectator's silver ring will appear on the wand. The ring falling from the wand to the left hand won't have to be shown or "flashed" later on. Practice the move on the stick once or twice to get the feel of it before performing the effect.

SCISSORS THROUGH

This scissors penetration will look impossible. It makes a very nice stage effect and involves two spectators. You need two five-foot lengths of rope, a pair of small scissors, and a ruler or wand.

Drape both pieces of rope over the ruler so that they hang down evenly (Fig. 62). Have the helpers each take one end of the ruler as you tie a simple knot in the two hanging ropes. Take one double strand in each hand and tie them together as if they were single strands of rope. In other words, cross the two right strands over the left ones and bring them up behind the ropes through the opening to form the knot. Tie it snugly onto the ruler. (Fig. 63.)

Pick up the scissors and thread one pair of strands through the thumb hole. Ask one of the spectators to hold both ends of that pair. Thread the other two strands through the other opening in the scissors. The second spectator is asked to hold that pair of ropes. Allow them to let go of the ruler and stand away from one another as far as the rope will allow. Step away from the rope a moment and take a look at the situation.

"Let's make this more impossible."

Take a single strand from each spectator and tie them together, returning the ends to their owners. Each spectator still holds two pieces of rope at this point. Remove the ruler. Move the scissors gently back and forth, taking it by the two blades. Loosen the top knots as you move the scissors. Then suddenly pull down on the blades.

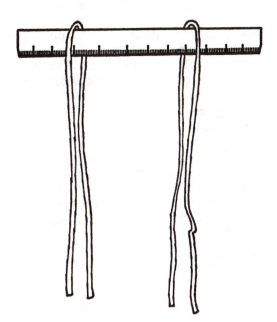

Fig. 62

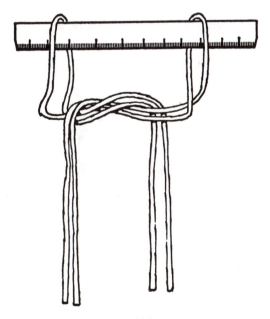

Fig. 63 111

The scissors will come loose from the ropes. The spectators will be left holding two ropes.

A small pair of scissors is best to avoid hangups around the curved ends. Experiment with a few to see which is best for you.

LINK IT

New York magician Dave Lederman can perform 40 minutes of beautiful and baffling magic using only a cord and a bracelet. Rings and ropes are common props used by the magician. You can use bangles and loops, cords and strings for any number of effects. Here is a startling penetration effect using a large metal ring and a five-foot length of soft rope.

Prepare the effect by secretly wrapping one end of the rope once around the ring. Have this on your table ready for the performance (Fig. 64).

Lift both the ring and rope with the right hand covering the twist. It will look as if the length of rope and the ring are separated in the right hand. The left hand takes the other end of the rope and ties a simple knot forming a large loop in the center of the rope.

Hold both ends of the rope firmly and throw the ring

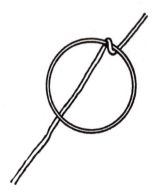

Fig. 64

through the large opening in the loop (Fig. 65). The weight of the metal ring will cause it to knot itself on the loop (Fig. 66). Pull the two ends of rope together to show that the ring is actually knotted in place.

This one takes a bit of practice, but once you have the knack, you'll do it every time.

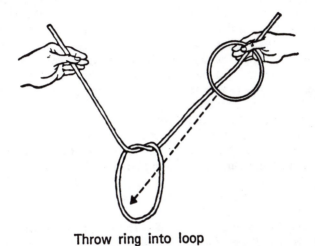

Throw ring into loop

Fig. 65

Fig. 66

WALK RIGHT THROUGH

Have two assistants help you off and on with your coat for this startling illusion. All you need to prepare is two lengths of rope, each about eight or nine feet long. Lay the ropes out evenly next to one another, and tie them together at the exact center with a piece of white cotton thread. (See Fig. 67.)

Fold the ropes so that you have two loops connected by the thread as shown. You have two folded loops that will look like two separate ropes. You will pick up the rope at the center so as to hide the connecting thread.

Remove your coat and drop one pair of ends (XX) down the right sleeve. Put your arm back into the sleeve and bring the ends out at your wrist. Place the other two ends (YY) into the left sleeve and bring them out to the left wrist.

Tie one rope from the right (X) to one rope at the left (Y) into a single knot (Fig. 68). Hand each spectator one pair of ends (XY).

> *"Gentlemen, I am now tied with the ropes around my body. If you will each take your ends and draw them back as far as you can, we will proceed. Pull the ropes taut. When I count to three, pull as hard as you can. The ropes should pass through my body. One ... two ... three!"*

The spectators pull the ropes, break the thread, and draw the ropes out of the coat. They are left holding the ends, and you are free behind the rope.

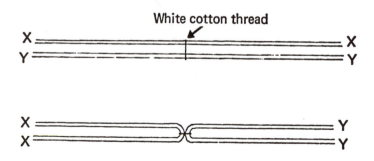

Fig. 67

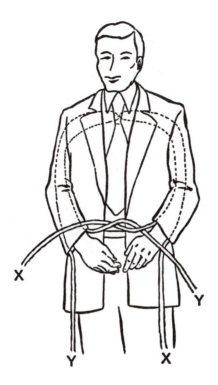

Fig. 68

COMEDY SHIRT TRICK

This one piece of business has made reputations for magicians over the years. Many were booked time and again just so their audiences could see this hilarious effect.

You need a confederate, a good friend who is a good sport and willing to join in the fun.

Before the show have him remove his jacket, vest, shirt and tie. Drape the shirt over his back. Button the collar and two top buttons of his shirt. Put his tie back on. If you have one, a clip-on

Fig. 69

bow tie is easier to remove later. Bring his shirtsleeves down along his arm and button the cuffs around his wrists. (Fig. 69.)

Replace his vest and jacket, and he will look normally dressed. The man will sit in your audience until you are ready to do the trick. No one must know that he is your assistant.

At the proper time ask for a volunteer and have your stooge come onstage. Pretend that you do not know him and introduce yourself. Ask him his name, what he does for a living, etc.

"Are you very nervous up here?"
He will shake his head "yes."

"Why don't you relax? Take your tie off."
He should seem reluctant to do this, so coax him a bit. Finally convinced, he will remove the tie and put it into his pocket.

"Are you more comfortable now?"
As you say this, he loosens the top buttons on his shirt. This is natural for him to do to make him look neater, since he has no tie.

"Are those gold cufflinks you're wearing?"
Remove the cufflinks or unbutton his cuffs.

He will become suspicious.

"What are you doing?"

You answer,

"Just trying to make you more comfortable."

He then replies,

"It's getting very warm up here."

That is your cue.

"How about some more air conditioning?"

Saying this, step behind him and grasp the back collar of his shirt. Pull it upward with a sudden sharp movement and the shirt will come right out of the coat. The laughs will come fast and furious. Have him grab for the shirt and run offstage.

"Let's have a nice round of applause for a good sport."

Never let on that he was your stooge. After the show, shake his hand and thank him, but have no more to do with him that evening.

ESCAPES

*If I got out too quickly the audience would
reason that escape was easy.*

Harry Houdini, quoted by Milbourn

**Harry Houdini, quoted by Milbourne Christopher,
HOUDINI: THE UNTOLD STORY**

ESCAPES AND RELEASES

Mention the name Harry Houdini and you will immediately
remind people of the great magician bound in chains and shackles.
He is always pictured in the mind for his ability to escape from
handcuffs and jails. He was the greatest escape artist in history.

But Houdini had been a magician first. He learned all the
principles of magic and developed his art, enabling him to evolve
the best escape methods possible in his time.

The escape trick could be considered a Penetration. The
chains and ropes seem to penetrate the magician's body. When he
escaped from a sealed trunk, Houdini called it "metamorphosis,"
which suggested a "transformation." Some people actually
believed that he would cause himself to dematerialize inside the
trunk and then materialize again outside.

Escape effects have fascinated people for centuries. There are
two forms of this trick. One is called the "escape." The magician
frees himself from his bonds of rope, chains, straitjackets, etc. The
second form is called a "release." Here the magician can reverse
the escape and bind himself up again.

Years ago magicians were tied and seated in small closed
cabinets called spirit cabinets. The doors were closed and from
inside the spectators would hear bells ringing and chains rattling.
Objects actually flew out over the top of the cabinet. When the

door was opened, the magician was seen inside still in his ropes. This was accomplished by the release, whereby the magician freed himself so that he could move the objects and then bound himself up again so as to be found in his original position.

It is unrealistic to teach most escape tricks to new magicians since they take a great deal of skill, strength, and discipline. We will cover a few of the fun escapes that are easy to perform.

KELLAR'S ROPE TIE

In 1865 the Davenport Brothers, two spirit mediums, startled all of England with their Spirit Cabinet act. The act was well received and played all over Europe. The American twin brothers amazed their audiences nightly by bringing "spirits" into their cabinet.

A few years later they hired an assistant, Harry Kellar, who was later to become one of the world's best-known magicians. Kellar almost believed the Davenports until one day he found that he could have a friend securely tie his wrists and that he could release one hand. The free hand could slip back into the knotted rope at will. Kellar never let on that he had discovered the Davenport secret.

Years later Harry Kellar used the principle in his own show, having developed a simple method. It is said that Kellar used several different ways to escape, but all the variations of the effect are still referred to as the Kellar Rope Tie.

Use a four- or five-foot length of sash cord or rope. Extend your left palm and allow someone to tie the rope around your wrist with a single knot. Bring both hands behind your back so that the back of your left hand is facing your body. Two ends dangle from the knot. Take the piece of rope at your left, nearest the pinky, and bring it around the back of your hand (Fig. 70).

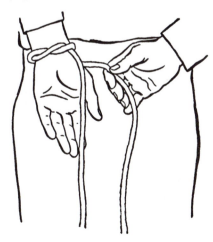

Fig. 70

Place the back of your right hand between the two pieces of rope, pressing the wrist against the knot (Fig. 71). Turn your body so that the spectator is facing your hands. Request that he or she tie another knot to bind both hands. Have one more knot tied with the same ends. Turn to face the audience, hands behind you.

The act of crossing the rope behind your hand gives you a bit of slack. This gives you about an inch of space between the knot and the right wrist.

If you uncross your hands, you will see that the right hand can be worked out of the loop quite easily. Once the right hand is out, you can use your fingers to loosen the knot around the left

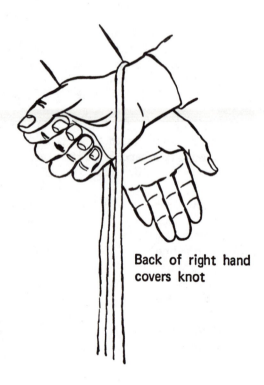

Back of right hand
covers knot

Fig. 71

wrist to effect your escape.

To perform this trick as a "release," merely remove the right hand and use it to hold your spectator's arm.

"Come a bit closer please."

Then bring the hand back into the loop and turn your back, asking the spectator,

"Would you tie another knot please?"

The audience will realize that you are free but very often the spectator onstage will not. This makes it a good piece of comedy.

Harry Blackstone Jr. has created the funniest and most entertaining comedy routine with his own version of this release trick.

COMIC ROPE ESCAPE

This is a fun piece of business that plays as funny in the living room as it does on the stage. You need two pieces of rope. One piece must be just small enough so that it cannot be tied around your ankles. The other piece is about five feet in length. Invite two helpers to assist you.

Sit yourself comfortably on a chair in the center of the stage. Both of your feet are flat on the floor. The small rope is at your left, and the long rope is in your hand. Pass the long rope under your legs just above the knees. Cross the rope in front of you, the right rope going over the left end. Have one assistant on each side of you take an end.

"Pull the ropes tightly, please."

This is only for effect since it does nothing. Your hands are now folded into fists. Place both hands together so that your wrists touch one another. Set your hands in your lap, placing the wrists directly over the crossed piece of rope. Ask one of the spectators to tie the rope around your hands.

"A few good knots please."

Ask the other spectator to add one more knot.

"Now that I am helplessly tied here, please remove your coat and cover my hands so that they are out of sight."

One of your spectators does this. The moment the coat is over your lap, turn both hands together toward your left. Both hands could now be released, but remove only your left hand. Bring it out from under the coat, and gesture to the man at your left.

"Please get that other piece of rope."

Place your hands under the coat again. The back of the left hand crosses over to the rope at your right side. Push the rope toward the left—now your hands are back in their original tied positions. Separate your knees slightly, and the rope looks even tighter. Speak to the man at your right.

> *"Can you lift the coat for a moment? I want to be sure the ropes are tight enough."*

This gives the audience a chance to see that the hands are still tied. Have the coat replaced, and this time slip the right hand out. Use it to instruct the man at your right.

> *"Can you tie the ropes around my ankles in a few good knots?"*

Put the right hand under the coat and remove the left hand. Beckon to the man at your left.

> *"Be a good fellow and give him a hand."*

Since the rope is too small, neither one can tie a knot. Remove both hands and take the small piece. Hold it up and tie in into a knot.

> *"If neither one of you guys can tie a simple knot, I'm afraid I can't do the trick. Thanks for your help."*

Return the coat, stand up, and step out of the ropes. Shake their hands as you send your spectators back to their seats. (Fig. 72.)

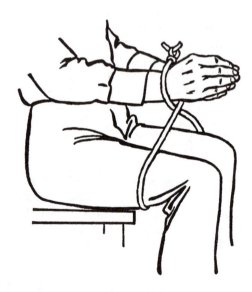

Fig. 72

LAUNDRY BAG ESCAPE

This principle can be used with a canvas mail bag, a potato sack, or the laundry bag that we describe. It is a simple escape that can be presented and made exciting with a bit of showmanship. Build up suspense and make this a feature in your show.

You will need a large sack that is big enough to hold a person. You'll also have to have a "feke," which is made of another piece of identical cloth. It should be eight or nine inches long and about the same width as the bag. Both bag and "feke" can be made from a dark-colored sheet. The word "Laundry" on the outer bag will be most effective.

Your assistant must rehearse with you to make the moves as smooth as possible. He or she will be wearing the smaller piece of cloth hidden in the jacket of his or her costume.

Show the sack and open it on the floor so that it will easy for your assistant to step into it. Help your assistant into the sack. Have him or her crouch down to the bottom of the bag. As you

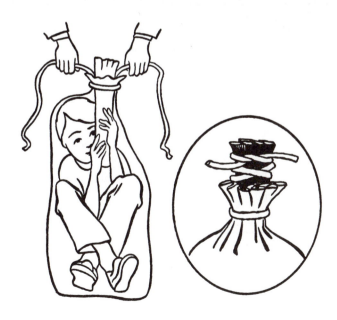

Fig. 73

pull up the top of the sack, the assistant secretly pushes the "feke" piece up to the top so that it is now in the center of the sack. You must bunch up the top of the sack. Pull a four-foot length of rope from your pocket and start to tie it tightly around the feke. After making a few knots, wrap the rope once around the actual top of the sack to keep it from opening. The bag will appear to be sealed at the top. (Fig. 73.)

If you have a screen, you can pull it in front of your assistant. If no screen is available, use a large blanket or sheet to hold up in front of the sack so no one can see what is really happening.

"My assistant will now attempt to escape from the sealed laundry bag in record time. At the count of three, he (or she) will be completely free. Watch!"

Music or a drumroll behind you will make the trick more exciting.

"One!"

As you start to count, the assistant will push up the cloth, enabling him (or her) to get out of the sack. He or she will hold the extra piece against the top of the sack as though it were still tied at the top.

"Two!"

At the count of *"Three!"* drop the blanket or remove the screen to reveal the assistant standing free and holding the tied sack up in the air for all to see.

This trick must be rehearsed very well so that there is enough time for the assistant to get out of the sack. Time your counting to coincide with the time it takes to escape.

LEVITATIONS AND SUSPENSIONS

. . . you knowe that it is doone with a long blacke haire of a woman's head, fastened to the brim of a groat, by meanes of a little hole driven through the same with a Spanish needle. . . .

Reginald Scot, DISCOVERIE OF WITCHCRAFT, 1584
Book XIII, Chapter XXIV

LIGHTER THAN AIR

Levitation and Suspension effects defy the laws of gravity. The covered body of the pretty Princess rises from the couch and gently floats upward into the air. That is levitation. Whenever an object or person floats freely in the air without any visible means of support, we call it Levitation.

The Broomstick Illusion is a modern-day Suspension. The lady's entire body is resting in space except for her elbow, which is suspended on the broom. The Suspension also defies the laws of gravity, but in this case the object is suspended on a single support.

Having logical minds, we know that with the levitation there must be some support somewhere. It's there, but not by "visible" means.

The famous Floating Ball trick, performed by such greats as Thurston, used black silk thread. The small ball was hooked onto the thread, causing it to move about the empty stage. The black art principle shows us that a black thread on a stage with a black backdrop or curtain becomes invisible. Black silk or nylon thread is still the magician's good friend when small objects must be made to levitate.

FLOATING BALL ILLUSION

With the house lights out and with only a dim blue light onstage, you can create a magical setting for this beautiful effect.

A drinking glass with a small silver ball inside sits on your table. This may be either a ping-pong ball painted silver with acrylic paint or a light styrofoam ball covered in silver foil. The metallic color will make the ball look heavier and help to hide the gimmick.

No one will see the gimmick, which consists of an 18-inch length of black silk or nylon thread. One end of the thread is wrapped a few times around the head of a straight pin. A dab of white liquid glue will cement the thread in place. The other end of the thread is wrapped tightly a few times around the lowest button of your shirtfront. It may also be attached to your belt buckle. The pin is stuck into your clothing at the right side of your body.

Soft but bright music in the background will help your presentation of this levitation.

Step to your table at your right and lift the glass with the left hand. With an upward motion toss the ball up and out of the glass, catching it with your right hand. Show it around so that everyone can see it.

Turn your body to the right as you set the glass back onto the table, mouth up. Transfer the ball to your left hand. The right hand drops out sight and secretly pulls the pin out of its hiding place. Bring both hands together at the same time, sticking the gimmick into the ball. Drop the ball into the glass. Make a few magical passes over the ball and glass. Pick up the glass with the right hand, setting it on the palm of the open left hand. Face the audience.

The glass is lowered to a position an inch or two below your waist level. Your left thumb and pinky hold the glass securely in place.

Gently move the glass straight out in front of your body. The thread will begin to tighten and the ball will rise up inside against the rear of the glass. Watch it rise until it reaches the rim of the glass. (Fig. 74.)

At this point take the ball away with your right hand, showing glass and ball in separate hands. Invert the glass and set it on the

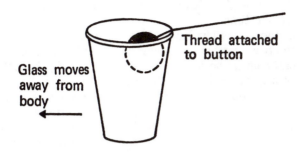

Thread attached to button

Glass moves away from body

Fig. 74

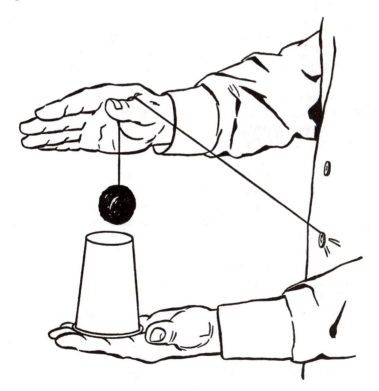

Fig. 75

left palm. Place the ball on top of the glass, lowering both to waist level. Move the glass toward the body about four inches away from your waistline.

Position your right hand, fingers apart, above the glass. Your right thumb moves between your body and the thread. Lift the hand gently until the thread becomes taut. (Fig. 75.) You may wiggle your right fingers for extra effect.

To cause the ball to float you must now lower the glass and move the right hand straight away from the body. Both hands move very slowly. The ball will float up into your waiting right hand. Separate both hands widely apart, breaking the thread. Toss the ball into the air and catch it in the glass. Take your bow.

It is important to note that when using styrofoam you must make sure that the ball isn't too large. The weight should not be heavy enough to fall off the pin. Experiment with a few different sizes until you find the right one. If you attach the thread to a small hook, you can also use a Christmas tree ornament ball, hooking the thread into the loop on top of the ball. Use this only for large stage work, as up close the loop is quite visible.

ELEVATOR RING ILLUSION

A bit of thread attached to your button on one end and a wand on the other end is all you need for this amusing routine. Use about 18 inches of thread as before. The wand is in your coat pocket so that you are unencumbered and free to do other tricks before this one.

"May I borrow a large finger ring, please."

Any ring will do as long as it will fit on the wand. If none is available, be prepared to use one of your own.

"Thank you. This is a nice ring. Is this your birthstone... plastic? I'm only kidding, it is a nice ring. It's an elevator ring, isn't it? You never heard of an elevator ring? Some people call it a floating ring. You've never heard of a floater on a ring? Let me show you what I mean."

Reach into your pocket and remove the wand, being careful not to break the thread. You must face your audience with no one on either side of you. The thread is at the top of the wand. Hold the wand down toward the bottom end and drop the ring so that it slides down the wand to your fingers. Hold the wand away from

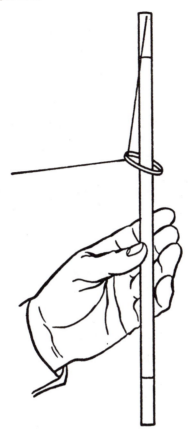

Fig. 76

your body until the thread is taut.

Do not move your hand too much, but slowly move your body backward. The ring will rise up along the wand mysteriously. (Fig. 76.) When it is almost at the top, command it to go down. Relax the tension on the thread, and the ring goes down. Bring the ring up again and remove it with your hand. Give it back to the spectator and proceed to the next trick, so that together you are doing a routine.

LIFTING WAND

This is a perfect follow-up trick for the Elevator Ring effect.

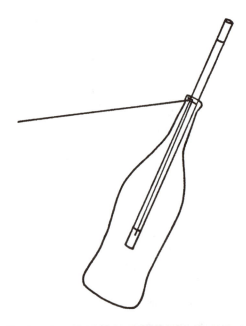

Fig. 77

Return the ring and use the same gimmick (thread on wand) as before.

Have an empty 12-ounce soda bottle on your table. A clear bottle is better than a colored one.

Place the wand into the bottle, but this time the thread end is at the bottom of the wand. The thread and wand go into the bottle together (Fig. 77).

"I learned this one in a supermarket. It is called Going Up, or The Story of Food Prices."

Make a few gestures over the bottle and cause the wand to rise up by moving the bottle gently away from you. Move your body back slightly at the same time so that your hand movement is not too obvious. Allow the wand to rise and fall a few times. Finally remove the wand. Break the thread and offer both wand and bottle to the spectator.

"Would you care to try it?"

Make sure that there is no trace of thread on his or her end of the wand when you hand it over.

SIMPLE SUSPENSION

You can have some fun with the simple Sucker Effect, in which the audience thinks they have caught you, when in fact you outsmart them. Children's performers love this kind of trick since it provides excitement and comedy.

A good many people can perform a simple suspension of a pencil, dinner knife, or wand. The easiest way is to hold the object so that it lies across the left hand. The left thumb holds it in place while the back of the left hand is shown to the audience. The right hand curls around the left wrist. The index finger of the right hand is extended in the left palm to hold the object in place as the thumb straightens out. Figs. 78 and 79 depict this.

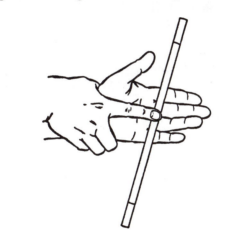

Fig. 78

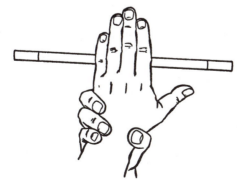

Fig. 79

Before doing this, secretly attach a thread to one end of the wand, pulling it along the wand so that it lies flat. Attach the other end of the thread to the other tip of the wand. The thread is almost taut.

First perform the simple version of the suspension. If no one says anything, offer to explain it. Then do so by showing the palm of the left hand with the index finger holding the wand in place. Take the wand off the palm for a moment.

Repeat the placement of the wand on the left palm, but do so with the palm facing your audience. However, as you do this your left fingers slip behind the wand so that they are between the thread and the stick. (Figs. 80, 81). Hold the right index finger as before, explaining that the right hand *"must never move from the wand."* As you say this, take the right hand away and point to the wand suspended on the left hand.

"Otherwise the wand will not be able to stay there."

You are suspending the wand while telling the audience that it can't be done. Slip the wand off the hand as you set it down.

"Please don't give away the secret of how it's done."

They thought they knew, but now you've suckered them.

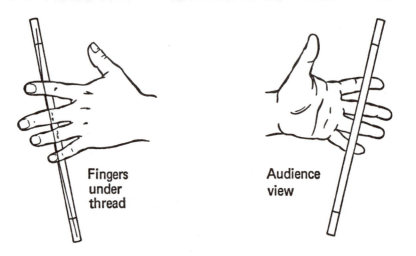

Fingers
under
thread

Audience
view

Fig. 80   **Fig. 81**

RISING CARDS

This effect was known as the "trick that mystified Herrmann," yet it is one of the oldest of card effects, dating back to the middle of the seventeenth century.

There are many ways of causing cards to rise from the pack, ranging from mechanical motors to the modern Devano type of mechanical deck. And yet the very oldest method is still most practical. Once again we go to our friend, the black silk thread.

In this version the card that is made to rise must be the top card. Later on you will learn that you can have a card selected from the deck freely and you can control it to the top of the pack.* Once the card is where you want it to be, you can reveal it however you like. For the "rising cards" you will need a drinking glass large enough to hold a deck of cards. You'll also need about a foot of black thread, a thumbtack, and a small dab of beeswax.

Prepare the trick by wrapping one end of your thread tightly around the thumbtack, which is the attached to the top of your table. If you do not want to ruin the table, you can use some strong cloth tape to hold it in place. The other end of the thread is attached to the beeswax. Tie the thread into a small knot, then roll the wax around the knot. In the absence of beeswax a small piece of cellophane tape will do. The thread will be on your table next to the glass, which is mouth down. Borrow or use your own deck of cards and have a card selected. Control the card to the top of the deck. This is done secretly so that no one can guess where the card is located.

Set the deck on the table next to the beeswax. The right hand picks up the dab of wax and places it on the bottom end of the top card. This is done without fanfare while the left hand is lifting the glass and turning it mouth up. Show the glass empty.

Set the glass on the table, mouth up. Lift all the cards and set them into the glass so that the bottom end of the top card will go into the glass first. The faces of the cards will be seen by the audience; the backs are facing you (Fig. 82).

"Please tell us the name of your card."
Someone will name the card—for example, the six of spades. Wave your hand over the deck and command the card to rise.

"Six of spades. Come up. Rise!"

*See page 160.

Thread attached to back of card and to table.
Move glass forward and card rises as shown.

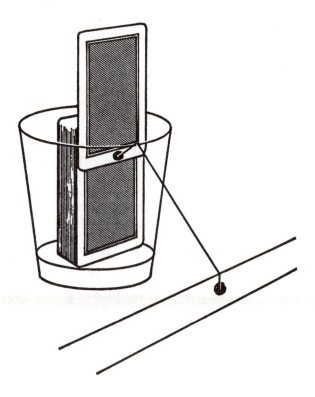

Fig. 82

Nothing will happen, of course. Now lift the glass straight up until
the thread is taut.

"I forgot to say 'please.' Six of spades, please come up."

Move the glass away from your body and the top card will mysteriously creep up. It will look as if it is coming from the middle of
the deck. Pull it out and push the wax off the card as you take
your bow.

Go back to the Floating Ball trick we learned earlier. You can
make a Rising Card gimmick by substituting the pin for some beeswax. Then you can attach a thread to the top card of a borrowed
deck and cause the card to rise as you did with the ball.

IMPROMPTU METHOD*

Since you are a magician, you should be able to perform your magic anytime and anywhere without having to rely on special props. With this version you can cause a card to rise from the deck without threads or wires. You will have a card selected, returned to the pack, and secretly brought to the top.

Hold the deck in your left hand, thumb on the inner end and fingers on the other side. The back of your hand should face your audience. Rub your right index finger on your sleeve as though trying to get some static electricity. Place your finger on top of the deck and say *"UP."*

Naturally, nothing will happen. Rub the index finger on the sleeve again. This time place the index finger on top of the deck, pressing the ball of the little finger against the middle of the top card.

As you lift the index finger, push the selected card up with the little finger. The selected card mysteriously rises from the deck. It will look as though it is coming out of the middle of the pack. (Fig. 83.)

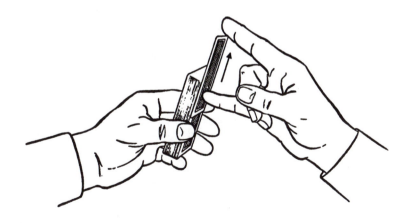

Fig. 83

---

*This trick is also described in *Magic With Cards*, by Frank Garcia and George Schindler.

THE PRINCESS FLOATS

If you had been alive in the 1870s, you would have seen the famous Princess Karnac Levitation performed by Harry Kellar. The young lady entered the stage dressed as a Hindu Princess. Kellar passed his hands over her face and she fell into a trance. The young lady was placed on a velvet-covered couch, and on the magician's command her body rose six feet into the air.

Our method of performing this grand illusion is not quite as complex as Kellar's. This can be done at a school or church auditorium and requires two assistants who are in on the trick. It may be presented as a serious illusion to close your show ... or as a comedy illusion.

You need to make some props. First, you must find a small bench or piano seat long enough for a young lady to lie on. You can use children for this if they are rehearsed. You'll also need two broomsticks and two matching pairs of sneakers or shoes. The last thing required is a large sheet that will cover the person you are levitating.

One person will play the part of the assistant from the audience. A short girl is best suited for this. She should be wearing one of the pairs of shoes or sneakers. You can pretend that she is a volunteer and not really your rehearsed assistant. One person will be needed to assist on stage. He or she must be available throughout the performance.

Prepare the stage with the bench set in the center. The broomsticks each have a single shoe or sneaker attached to one end. The length of the sticks will depend upon the size of the girl you are using (we'll assume it is a girl). The broomsticks and their shoes are on one end of the bench. The bench is covered with the sheet so that one end drapes over the front.

"For this grand illusion I will require the assistance of a young man or lady of relatively light weight. How about that young lady there? Would you be so kind as to help us with the miracle?"

Point to the girl you will use. She is sitting in the audience so that the act seems unrehearsed. She pretends she doesn't know anything about the trick. As soon as she is on the stage, ask her name and introduce her to the audience. Have your assistant come out from backstage. Introduce the two of them.

Ask the girl to stand behind the bench. You and your assistant each take one end of the sheet and lift it so that the girl is out of sight for a moment.

> *"Please lie down on the bench, head on one side and feet on the other."*

The girl straddles the bench, with her head on one side. She will quietly lift the broomsticks, one in each hand. She brings her back down to rest on the bench as in Fig. 84.

> *"At my command you will float."*

You and your assistant cover her body with the sheet.

> *"Rise!"*

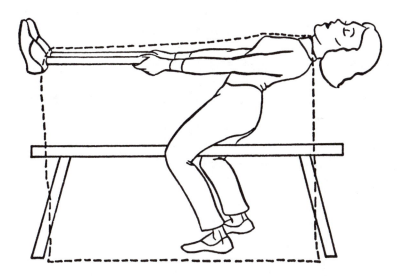

Fig. 84

As you say this, the girl will gently lift her body off the bench. The audience sees her levitating (Fig. 85). Your arms are spread apart as you stand behind the bench.

Once she is off the bench your assistant carefully pulls the bench away from the girl. Her feet are apart so that the bench will easily slide back behind her head and away from the sheet.

Once the bench has been removed, your body and arms will sway from left to right. Have the girl rock back and forth so that her body will appear to sway in the same direction.

"*Move.*"

On hearing your command, the girl will start taking very tiny

Fig. 85

steps, walking ahead of her, still in crouched position. It will look as if she is floating away.

At this point walk out in front of her.

"Before she floats away, I'd like to say good night and thank you."

Have the curtain closed. Get rid of the extra sticks, and then all three of you come out front to take your bows. Send the girl back to her seat.

Once the audience has been completely baffled by the original levitation, you can change the ending to a hilarious comedy exposure that will be talked about for a long time. Clowns do this one in the circus.

After you say *"Move,"* have the girl walk off the stage in her crouched position. But you must place one foot on the sheet so that it comes off as she is walking. In this way the audience sees her with the shoes and the laughs will begin. Pretend not to have noticed this, then do a double-take and shrug. *"How else?"*

MINDREADING AND ESP

To tell one without confederacie what card he thinketh.

Reginald Scot, DISCOVERIE OF WITCHCRAFT, 1584
Book XIII, Chapter XXVII

MENTALISM

Tricks involving mind reading or ESP are put into the category called Mentalism. Many people would like to believe that extra-sensory perception (ESP) is a real and workable possibility. As long as I cannot disprove its existence I will always keep an open mind. But as a magician I find that all the experiments I have ever seen in this field can be duplicated by common "magical" means.

You will see that the mechanics of the mental effects are quite simple to master. It will be the presentation of those effects that will make your act interesting and believable. The outcome of the trick is important to the spectator. Always use simple props that do not distract the audience. Speak with a degree of authority and present your material in a clear, almost serious manner. A little light humor cannot hurt, but it is very hard to blend the two for the maximum of effect.

It is important to remember that when you present effects of this nature, you must *not* claim any special powers. Never claim that you are psychic or are a mind reader. People may believe that you have the talent, but if you say you are doing something that you are not, you are a charlatan and not an entertainer. Keep your experiments short and simple. Offer logical or scientific-sounding explanations. Read as much as possible on the subject so that you can discuss ESP with some degree of knowledge.

Concentrate!

Newspaper Test

Obtaining information is the first step to learning the technique of mind reading. If you ask a man to think of a single number, idea, or word on a page, he holds this information in his head. Since we have no known method of reading his thoughts, we must think of an alternate way to get this information. In this case you will ask the spectator to write it down.

"Can you picture the word in your mind as clearly printed as though it were written on a blackboard? Perhaps you should write it down so you can picture it better."

Then the spectator writes his thought so as to be able to envision it better, and he keeps the paper. He will feel secure that the information is still a secret known only to himself. What the spectators do not know is that magicians or mentalists have ways of seeing that information. In this case we'll use carbon paper.

Your table is set with a blackboard or small slate and some chalk. You will also need a few lightweight pieces of paper about 4 x 6 inches in size, a good sharp pencil or ballpoint pen, and a specially prepared newspaper.

Use a few sheets of today's newspaper folded in half from the bottom up. Fold it in half again the other way so that you have a square package. Your spectator will soon use this paper for a writing surface. Lift the top right corner of the top sheet of paper. Behind this page you will cement a square of a good quality carbon paper. On the facing page (page 3) glue a small piece of clean white paper. The paper and the carbon should line up so that they are both in the same position under the top sheet. (Figs. 86, 87).

The newspaper is also on the table, and now you're ready to begin your experiment. You will note that when doing mentalism we refer to all of our tricks as experiments. This allows the spectator to think that there is a science involved.

Open your newspaper so that the entire front page is seen. Invite a spectator up to help. We will assume it is a gentleman.

"Sir, there are thousands of words printed in each newspaper every day. Here is today's paper. Please take a good look at this page and scan the words. How many words would you say there are? Too many to count. Please allow your eyes to travel about the page until one word strikes your fancy. Have you found one word on that page that you can relate to? Please think only of that word."

Carbon and white paper in alignment

Fig. 87

Fig. 86

Fold the newspaper in half and then in half again so that the gimmicked side is at your right. Pick up a piece of plain white paper. Set it directly over the spot where the carbon is hidden. Hand the spectator a pencil or pen along with the newspaper.

"Please print that single word carefully and clearly on the piece of paper. Make it as legible as possible so you can read it again when needed. Keep the paper and fold it twice so the word is hidden inside the paper."

Take the newspaper and pencil back. As you walk to your table, open the paper and refold it again, taking a good look at the carbon impression inside. Toss the paper aside. Once you know the word you can do the build-up. Lift the slate and chalk and walk well away from the spectator.

"Please hold the paper to your forehead, sir. I intend to receive some of the mental signals your mind will emit. Concentrate!"

Do not reveal the word immediately. Take it step by step as though you were actually receiving mental images.

"Please picture the word carefully spelled out as it is on your paper."

Let us assume the word is "patriot." Here is how you might reveal it.

"I get the letter T. Is there a letter T in that word please? There is? Good. Concentrate on the other letters please. I seem to be getting the T again. Think of another letter please. I get an O and the T again. Is there more than one T in the word? There is. I get the name Pat . . . no, it's coming clearer . . . Patriot. Is that the word please?"

While you are talking, you are writing on your slate. Write the word "Patriot" so that all can see that you are right.

"Keep the paper with you at all times, sir, so that you can remember this once-in-a-lifetime experience."

Gypsy Method

When performing mental effects for only a few people, you can obtain information by a method known as the Center Tear. It was used years ago by Gypsies and fortune-tellers and in recent years by mentalists. In this case have the person write his thought on a piece of paper that you give him. The paper should be a square of no more than three inches. There are three steps in obtaining the information you need. First is to make sure that the spectator writes his word exactly where you tell him to.

You can fold the sheet in half, then in half again, so that when opened the crease will be in the exact center of the paper. You can make a small circle there to make it simpler. Instruct the spectator to write his thought in the exact center of the paper.

"Please print the name of some person who is close to you. A person whom I do not know. Just write the first name in the center of the paper."

Notice that you are giving the spectator exact instructions. Do it casually so that you do not command but rather ask that your wishes be carried out.

The second step has been made a bit easier since you have already folded the paper.

"Please fold the paper so that the writing is hidden inside."

Have an ashtray and some matches handy. A good setting is for you all to be seated around a table. Take the folded paper from the spectator with your right hand. Hold the paper by the top corner where the folds meet. Your thumb is against the corner, your index finger on the other side. The paper is folded to your left. Use the left hand to help you tear the paper vertically in half. (Fig. 88.) Place half in the left hand directly in front of the piece in your right hand, under your index finger.

Turn the papers a half-turn to the right and tear all the pieces in half again (Fig. 89). As you put the left-hand pieces in front of the right pieces, your right thumb must slide the topmost piece to the right. The single square (X) is under your right thumb, and the rest of the pieces are in the left hand. Tear the balance of the pieces in half directly above the ashtray and allow them to flutter down. You will retain the single piece (X) in the right hand. (Fig. 90.)

Hand the spectator the matches with your left hand as the right hand casually drops to your lap. If you put your thumb into one of the folds and push it upward, the small square opens like an umbrella. This tiny square will have all the information.

"Please burn the pieces. Light the match carefully and make sure all the paper is in ashes. Watch the smoke as it rises."

Close your eyes and place your hand over them on your forehead so it looks like you are in deep concentration. Do not attempt to read the information as yet. When you are ready, open your eyes under cover of your hand and you will be able to look down into your lap secretly.

Open your eyes and pretend to be getting a picture of a

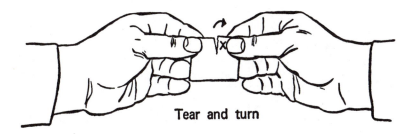

Tear and turn

Fig. 88

Fig. 89

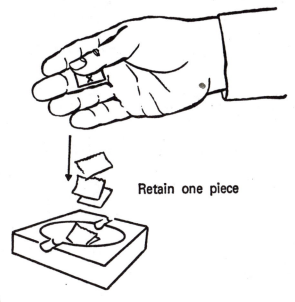

Retain one piece

Fig. 90

person. Let us say that the name was Helen. Do not reveal the name, but begin to fish for a description.

"This person has very unusual eyes. I believe they are brown." You have an almost 50-50 chance of guessing right since brown and blue eyes are most common. But do not worry if you are wrong, you can always ask.

"What color are they, please? I picture a very pretty woman."

No one will admit his friends are not pretty.

"She has a Greek name. Is the person whom you are thinking about named Helen?"

A bit of blarney helps the mentalist. Make your description as interesting as possible. If you are wrong, ask the correct information. The spectator has a short memory and will only remember the correct information you gave, forgetting your guesses.

Four at a Time

Here is a simple tear enabling you to get four pieces of information all at the same time. This is done seated at a table. Have your spectators in front of you, also seated. You will need a piece of lightweight paper such as onionskin typing paper for this one.

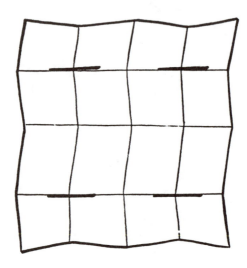

Fig. 91

A sheet about 4 x 6 inches is fine. The paper is folded in half once, then again the other way. This package is folded the same way once more. Four folds are made.

When opened, you will see sixteen little boxes. Draw lines at the four places shown in Fig. 91.

To make your test more interesting ask for each of four spectators to write different thoughts. For example, the first person will think of a name, the second person will draw a simple design, the third one will write his social security number, and the last one will write the name of a country or city in the world.

As each one finishes writing, he or she is to hand the paper to the next one. After all have written their information, have the paper refolded. This gives you a tight little bundle which you will tear exactly as before.

When opened in your lap, the extra section will consist of four small bits. Two are going to be face up and two face down, so after each reading you must secretly turn the paper over in the lap.

One burning will offer four good readings, which is enough for any evening. Have fun with this one.

BOOK TEST

Very powerful mental effects are called blockbusters, because they have great impact on an audience. This book test is a special favorite of mine since it uses a common math principle along with a good deal of showmanship.

Use a phone book that has more than 900 pages. If your own book does not have enough pages, use one from another larger city such as Chicago, New York, Los Angeles, etc. The phone company will supply you with one at no cost. You'll also have to do a little research.

Open the book to page 99. Use the first column on the left side of the page and count down 18 names. Record the eighteenth name and corresponding phone number. Write or print it neatly on a 3 x 5 index card or paper pad. Do the same with page 198. The eighteenth name in left column is what you need. Repeat the process with the following page numbers: 297-396-495-594-693-792-891. Your chart will look like the one in Fig. 92. You will notice that the digits of these numbers always total eighteen. The center digit is a nine and the two outer digits total nine.

Paste or tape the chart on the second page of a small memo pad. Use the type that has a foldover cover so you can keep the

99-	Atlas, Louis.	799-0518
198-	Brooks, Betty.	369-3221
297-	Computers, Inc.	227-8957
396-	Edelberg, A.	724-0478
495-	Gale, John C.	861-8937
594-	Harris, Robert.	233-7866
693-	Johnson, Fred.	283-3082
792-	Lefkowitz, E.	674-2440
891-	McCall & Co.	580-6339

Fig. 92

chart hidden until you need it. Prepare your table with a few pencils, a paper pad, a piece of chalk, and a small slate or blackboard. Your gimmicked pad is also on the table.

Invite one assistant on the stage to help you. Assure the audience that this person is a stranger or one who did not plan or rehearse anything with you. *"We did not prearrange anything, is that true?"* He will answer honestly.

Offer the spectator the pad and pencil.

"Will you please go down into the audience and choose any person you wish to assist you."

When he or she is now in the audience, offer the following instructions.

"Please ask your helper to write down any three-digit number, making them three different digits please."

Wait until this has been done.

"Now take that number to any other person in the audience. Have that person reverse the three digits so that we have two numbers. For example if the first number was 321, the second number is 123."

Wait until this is done. (Fig. 93.)

$$
\begin{array}{r} 983 \\ -389 \\ \hline 594 \end{array}
\qquad
\begin{array}{r} 624 \\ -426 \\ \hline 198 \end{array}
$$

Fig. 93

"Bring the pad to someone else, please. Will that person please subtract the smaller number from the larger number so that we arrive at an answer."'

This takes another few moments.

"Only two people now know what that number is. If my assistant will return to the stage, keeping the result hidden, we can proceed."

Hand the spectator a phone book when he or she returns.

"This book is a standard phone book from (name of the city) which has thousands of names and phone numbers recorded. Please take the book and turn to the page number that matches the result of our random subtraction. If the result was 100 you would look at page 100, if your answer was 675 you would turn to page 675. Do this please, and put the pad in your pocket."

While your spectator is looking for the correct page, you can determine if he or she has chosen a low, middle, or high number. The results of the subtraction as described will always give you one of the nine key numbers we prepared earlier. This is called a "force" since we know the result beforehand and force the spectators to produce it.

A tiny ink mark on page 900 will help you estimate if your spectator is looking at the beginning, middle, or end of the series. You will usually be able to guess within three numbers of the series.

"Do you have that page? Please look at the page number again. Add all the digits of that number so you have a random total. For example, if you are on page 102, the digits would add up to three. Have you got the idea?"

This is another "force," and not a random selection at all. All the numbers in our series to total eighteen.

"Please look at the left-hand column of your names and count down that many names. If your total was twenty-five, you will look at the twenty-fifth name. Have you got it?"

Hand the helper a piece of chalk and the slate.

"Since no one in the audience can see what you are looking at, please print that person's name and phone number on the slate. Do not let me see it."

Turn your back to the spectator, but not to the audience. Turn so that you are facing stage right or stage left. Take your special pad and a pencil with you as you walk away from the spectator.

"I will not be looking. Please turn the blackboard so that everyone can see what is taking place. I shall attempt to read

your thoughts to determine the single name from the thou-
sands in that phone book. Please concentrate on the name."
Open your pad to page two so that you can see your chart. If you
were able to get a good estimate of the page selected, you can start
with a close guess. If you think it was a low number, start off with
one of the first three names (the middle numbers are around 400-
500). The lower the page number, the lower the name in alpha-
betical order. Select a name that corresponds with your guess.
Follow our chart as an example.

Let us assume he opened to the middle section of numbers.
You would guess at E-G or H.

"Concentrate on only the first letter of the person's last
name. Are you thinking? (Pause) *I believe I am getting the*
letter G. Am I correct, please?"

If you hit it correctly, you have an easy task and can proceed with
the rest of the revelation. If you did not guess right, do not des-
pair. You can ask.

"I'm sorry, I can't receive that one. What was the first letter
please?

Now that you know the first letter of the last name, you know
exactly which name was written. Let us assume that you miscalcu-
lated and he or she tells you it is letter L.

"L? I can't get that picture. I still get a G. Let us concentrate
on a few of the other letters. Do I perceive the letter W?
Thank you. I believe there is a W and an O. Do not tell me if
I am right or wrong. I get a K. . . . It's not quite clear. May
we go to the numbers, please? Concentrate on the phone
number . . . . I see a 6 or a 7. . . . I see both . . ."

Scribble on your pad as you speak. Actually, make the noise with
your fingernail and do not write on the pad at all.

"The number is 674- . . . 2 . . . 4 . . . another 4 and a zero.
Am I correct?"

You'll get applause here, but raise your hand to stop it.

"Look at the name again please. I see an L and an E. . . .
There is a K and an F . . . Lefkowitz, the name is Lefkowitz,
am I correct?"

Close the pad and put it into your pocket. Hold up the blackboard, thank your helper, and take a well-deserved bow. You've
done a fine acting job and one that merits an award.

When trying to recreate the test, your spectators will forget
the numbers, and some will almost swear that the book and page
were chosen at random by the spectator. Accept all the applause
and let them think what they will.

Magazine Mystery

This book test involves a little bit of cheating, but it is very clever and takes less time to discover your information.

Prepare three identical copies of a popular magazine. Any of the national news magazines would be good. Remove two of the covers very carefully. You can do this by removing the staple. Re-cover these two copies with two covers of the same magazine of different months. Staple or paste the covers over the front pages. The three magazines will all appear to be different issues but are really all the same. Discard the rest and keep the three on your table until you are ready to perform.

Invite someone to participate and bring him or her to the stage.

"Thank you for your help. Have we ever met before? Did we arrange this experiment before the show? Good. I'm going to use a magazine for an experiment in telepathy."

Hand the lady or gentleman all three copies.

"I'm going to let you select any one of these so you can see that you have a free choice. Take one, please, and we will discard the others."

Toss the unused copies on the table. Ask your spectator to move away from you.

"Please step to the other side of the platform so that I cannot see your magazine."

Stay at your table for the beginning of the test.

"Please open the book to any page you like. You may change your mind as often as you wish. Have you decided on any one page? I have not influenced you in any way, have I? You may still choose another page if you so desire."

The build-up will dispel any thoughts of a force or collusion.

"Will you look at the page number, please. Total the digits. What page are you on please?"

As soon as you know the page number, you can "read" the spectator's mind. Pick up one of the magazines on the table. We'll assume that page 78 was selected. You turn your magazine to that page as if you were going to explain what you need.

"Okay. Here is page 78. You would add those digits, eight and seven, which gives you 15. You will then start at the top left of the page and count in that many words. Stop at the fifteenth word."

As you explain it, you look at the fifteenth word (or whatever word it comes out to be), remember it, and also any picture or ad that is on the page. Toss your magazine aside and pick up a slate.

"Do you have that word in your magazine? Good. Please concentrate and I will see if I can receive your thoughts."

Reveal the word in a dramatic manner, letter by letter. For example, if the word is "America," you could start with some of the letters.

"I get an M and an A. This is a name, I believe. . . . I'm getting a picture. I see an outline of a map. Is this a city or country? I get an AME . . . America. . . ."

Use a little blarney again to reveal the word. Do not stop there. If there is an ad or a picture on the page, you can describe it.

"Is there a photo or picture on the page? Please draw that picture in your mind."

Draw a crude sketch on your slate and finally reveal it by describing it. Then ask to see the magazine firsthand. Show it to your audience and take your bows.

PREDICTIONS

Wouldn't it be interesting if you could know what was going to happen before it happens? If you had "precognition," you would be able to predict the future. For centuries fortune-tellers have been making predictions even though there isn't a single scientific method of doing this. People would love to believe that clairvoyance and ESP exist and are therefore impressed by a good demonstration of this ability.

There are only two ways for a magician to be able to make an accurate written prediction. He must either write his prediction and switch it for another one after the fact, or he must have some advance knowledge or information. The second way is easier, since we have the "force" working for us.

Ask someone to give you a number between one and nine. He will probably say "seven." This is one of many psychological forces the mentalist can use to force a reply. Here are a few more that I described in *Magic with Everyday Objects*.

Instructions	Average Response
"Name a Color!"	"Red" (second choice, "Blue")
"Think of a vegetable"	"Carrot"
"Name a ferocious animal"	"Lion" (second choice, "Tiger")

When forced to offer a quick response, most people select the most obvious. Try this one. Ask that your spectator draw a simple geometrical figure, *"such as a square or hexagon."*

Since you have already named a few, your spectator will think of a different figure and will usually come up with a triangle. Knowing that people respond this way can help you with your predictions. If you had a triangle drawn in advance, you could compare your drawings and your prediction would come true.

On your business card write the words *"I knew you'd pick 3."* Show your spectator the clean back of the card and write the numbers 1—2—3—4. Then ask him to *"Pick a number. What number is it?"*

Because you need a fast reply, he will most likely pick 3, at which time you show him your card with the correct prediction on it.

Number Forces

We used the Nine Principle in our Book Test effect and we saw that we can force the number 18 as a result of reversing three digits, subtracting one number from another, and totaling the digits in the result. If we carried the addition of the digits one step further, we could force the number 9. Add the 1 and 8 of the number 18 and we have the 9.

If you knew the ninth card from the top of the deck, you could predict that card in advance by using the "force." You could vary it and predict the eighteenth card the same way.

Carrying our numbers a step further, we can have the result of the subtraction reversed and totaled for a larger number. We know that by subtracting one reversed number from the other, we must have one of nine results. Let's assume we had number 198. We then ask that this number be reversed and the two new numbers be added together: $198 + 891 = 1089$

In almost every case the answer is the same 1089. There is a single exception. $(99 + 99 = 198)$ You can now use this for another book test predicting the ninth word on page 108 or the eighteenth word on page 1089. You must ask the spectator, *"Do you have a four-digit answer?"* If he replies *"No,"* you know he selected numbers to total 198. Merely ask him, *"Do it again please, we need a high number,"* or *"You're thinking of number 198. Please do not think of the numbers. I do not wish to know what they are. Try it again with other numerals, please."*

Star Prediction

If you know that you're going to be performing at a specific place and time, you can send your prediction to someone a week in advance of that appearance. It will make the actual performance more exciting and much more unbelievable.

Draw a five-pointed star on a piece of cardboard, fold it in half, and place it in an envelope. Seal the envelope and mark the outside, *"To be opened on March 15 at 8 P.M."* Write another note with instructions that tell the receiver to keep the prediction in his safe and let no one touch it until you open it on the night of the appearance. Ask that he sign his name and the date he received it on the face of the envelope. Place both note and prediction in a larger envelope and send it registered mail to the person booking you or the chairman of the committee who hired you. Naturally the date and time are the same as your appearance.

On the evening of the performance ask that the envelope be brought forward and kept in a place where it can be viewed by everyone. You will then make a big deal of this, explaining that the envelope was mailed in advance, that no one tampered with it, that the person who holds it did not conspire with you, and so on.

Now for the effect. You'll need a small package of cards made up of postcard stock paper. You can buy this at a stationer's or make up a few out of cardboard. The cards should be about 2 x 3 inches in size. I suggest about 10 of them. A felt-tip marker, some coin envelopes large enough to accommodate the cards, a rubber band, and a small stand or shelf to display some of the cards are needed.

Before the show secretly prepare four of the cards. With the same felt-tip pen you will use later, draw a star design on each of these cards. Put the four cards on top of the others with the star side down so that they cannot be seen. Circle the cards with a rubber band. Make a tiny mark on the corner of the topmost card so that you know which side is up. Turn the package upside down and leave it on the table with the coin envelopes.

Invite one of your spectators to come up to assist you.

"Are you familiar with ESP? Some years ago Duke University conducted studies in this field trying to determine ways and means to transmit thought waves. They used a collection of different symbols to help them."

Pick up the cards, remove the rubber band, and deal off three or four cards to the spectator.

*"We're going to use a few cards. Will you look at them,
please? They're just cardboard."*

Take the cards back, place them on top of the stack. Now turn to
your table for a marking pen and casually turn the cards over in
your hand. The four prepared cards are now on top of the pack in
your hand.

*"I'm not a great artist, but I'll try to draw some of the
designs they used at Duke. First there was a circle."*

Draw the circle and then remove that card so that no one can see
the underside and lean it against your stand. A large book can be
propped up for a stand. The audience sees the design but not the
back of the card.

"They also used a cross."

Draw this one and again place the card on the stand. Do the same
with the next two designs, a square and a set of wavy lines (see
Fig. 94 for the way the lines are patterned). Pick up the last card
and turn it over a few times so that people can see it blank. Do not
say that it is blank, but pause,

"I forget the last one. Oh yes, a star."

Draw the star and set it on the stand with the other designs. At
this point the stand has four different designs showing with stars
on their backs. The last one is the star alone. (Fig. 94.)

Starting with the circle, place the cards one at a time into
each of the coin envelopes. The flap of the envelope opens so that
it faces the audience. Make sure that no one sees the back of the
design cards and that no one sees through the coin envelopes.
A good manila envelope is opaque. As each card is sealed in, hand
the envelope to the assistant. Pick up the last card and, as you place
it into its envelope, flash the back. It is blank so that once again the
audience will believe they were all blank.

*"You now have five designs. There is one chance in five that
I have in guessing which one you will select. I will ask you to*

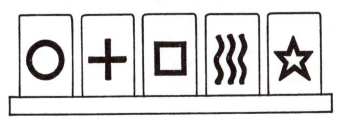

First four designs have star symbols on the back.
Star at right has regular back design.

Fig. 94

take the envelopes behind your back and mix them up. Keep only one for yourself and give me the others."

When he returns the other envelopes, put them in your pocket.

"We won't need these. Before the show, at least one week ago, I made a prediction that was mailed to (name of the person). He has that prediction with him. Please, sir, bring it up onto the stage. Have you and my helper prepared anything together? You did not know that we would conduct this experiment. I have my prediction there and will not touch it. May I have the small envelope, please?"

Take the coin envelope back and turn it so that the flap is facing you. Gently tear it open and look inside. There is one single chance that it is the real star. If it is, hand the envelope back to the helper. If not, continue by slowly removing the card. The audience will see the star. Press the card against the coin envelope so that the envelope covers the design on the back. Hold it up.

"This gentleman selected the star."

Point to the other man and dramatically command that he open his envelope.

"Show us what you have inside. It is the star!"

As you speak, casually place the small card and envelope into your pocket and take your bow.

This effect is one that I use in my lectures for my fellow magicians. A variation of this method was described in my article for the *M-U-M* Magazine in July 1974. It is suggested that each time you present the effect you use a different prediction design.

Answering Sealed Questions

In vaudeville days mind readers featured the Question Answering act. A turbaned young lady sat at a table next to a crystal ball and supposedly answered questions that were mentally transmitted to her from the audience. People wrote out their questions, which were folded and then burned in a bowl onstage. The "medium" concentrated, offering advice and answering questions she received through "thought transmission."

This is a great stunt for a party or a group of about 10 people or more. You can do it alone and impromptu. All you need is some pencils and a paper pad or any paper that can be torn into slips of the same size. Hand the slips out to every member of the crowd. Borrow a hat or a deep bowl.

"I'd like everyone to think of some question that you would like me to answer. Anything that is not too personal to reveal to these nice people. Please sum up your questions so that you have only two or three key words in your mind. Print those few words on your papers and fold them in half. Fold them once again in half the other way. Let me know when you are through."

The writing will take a bit of time. Use this time to prepare your table. Make sure it has a cloth and a chair behind it. Set it apart from the crowd so that no one will be seated next to you or behind you.

When they are all set, pick up the bowl and walk around the room, collecting the slips of paper. Have each person drop his question into the bowl. After all are collected, walk back to your table. As you go back, transfer the bowl from one hand to the other and steal a single question. There is plenty of time to do this casually and without any furtive moves. As you sit down, drop the extra slip in your lap. Set the bowl to one side of your table and drop both hands into your lap, looking straight at the audience. Tell them what is to happen.

"I will attempt to gather your thoughts and answer your questions one at a time. With your help I will answer as many questions as possible."

While you are talking, you are secretly opening the slip in your lap. Set it on the lap so that you can steal a peek at it to get your information. Hold one hand on your forehead for a moment as you did with the "center tear." Bring both hands to the table. Remove a single question from the bowl and press the folded slip to your forehead. You are going to answer the question that you just read in your lap.

After the question has been answered, casually unfold the slip as if to verify it. What you are actually doing is reading the next question. You will always stay one question ahead of the one on your forehead. This is called the "one-ahead" system of answering questions.

Continue until you have done about four or five, then stop. Get rid of the extra slip on your lap by crumpling it and adding it to the others open on your table. Crumple all of them together and cast them aside.

By having the ideas summed up, you can get the theme without having to read long sentences. Asking your spectators to print the thoughts makes them easier for you to read. The technique of "cold readings" or answering questions will come by experience. Your answers are vague and in general terms. With proper practice you can elicit the entire question and all the information you need from the spectators themselves. Try to have fun with them.

Here are a few sample questions and answers you might get.

Q: Color. Car

A: *I see a large object, it is not very clear, all I can see is wheels. It's a car. Who is asking about a car, please raise your hand. I get a picture of a beautiful black car. No wait. I can't quite make out the color. All I know that it is a color that you like. Thank you.*

Q: Rich

A: *Someone is asking about money. The question concerns a person close to you. You are much interested in wealth. Please let me answer this way. Happiness and your personal health are most important.*

Q: Baby. Name

A: *I am receiving messages from someone concerned with a child. It is a very small child. It is a baby. I'm not sure if it is newly born or about to be born. Which is it?* (You'll get an answer.) *Not yet born? Please do not worry about the child, madam.   He or she will have a fine name and one that will some day be famous.*

If you find a question that really stumps you, try to think for a moment, read the key word, and then answer it this way.

"The answer here is a very delicate matter. Please see me privately afterward and we can discuss it."

Never advise people on matters of money or their marriages. Keep away from serious questions. Some people may believe you and get into trouble as a result of your answers.

For extra fun you can have a confederate in on the trick. In this way you do not have to steal a question, merely make one up and have your confederate say that it was his or her question. You can still get one ahead that way.

MAGIC WITH CARDS

*Of cards with good cautions how to avoid cou-
senage therein: speciall rules to conveie and
handle the cards, and the maner and order how
to accomplish all difficult and strange things
wrought with cards.*

**Reginald Scot, DISCOVERIE OF WITCHCRAFT, 1584
Book XIII, Chapter XXVII**

CARD TRICKS

Card tricks are in a category all by themselves. You can perform
the standard vanishes, productions, restoration, and levitations
with cards. You can also provide good entertainment of the "pick
a card" variety. There are more books on card magic than there
are devoted to any other kinds of tricks. The title of this chapter is
also the title of a book I wrote with Frank Garcia, *Magic with
Cards*. We described 113 no-skill card tricks that can be done with
a regular deck. Our book is still outselling most other books on
general magic. One of the reasons for the strong interest in card
magic is that you will always find a deck of cards available. You
can borrow it to perform your magic impromptu, anywhere at any
time. There are so many thousands of variations of card effects
that to describe them all would take many volumes.

The card magic we will cover in this chapter will be concerned with self-working effects that do not take many hours of
practice and sleight of hand. I believe that the new magician
should be able to start entertaining with his magic immediately. In
this way the enthusiasm will not fade and the excitement of performing magic will stimulate him to higher forms of the art. Learn
your manipulative skills and develop your craft. But while you are
working on it, be ready to perform simpler effects.

The average "pick a card" trick is broken into two component parts. The first part is known as the Location, which is the secret way the magician gains the identity of the selected card. The "location" is the magician's work, and the spectator must have no idea of what is involved.

The second part of the trick is called the Revelation, which is the way the magician reveals the name of the card that was selected. It is the Revelation that is the most important part as far as the viewer is concerned.

The showmanship, drama, comedy, surprise, and impact of the trick is provided in the Revelation part. The presentation is the "magic," and it is the Revelation that requires the showmanship. You may remember how easy it was to get information for the mind reading trick, but it was the impact that you gained with good acting ability that made the trick effective.

Your Card Is in Chicago

The most effective card magic is done with a regular deck of playing cards that can be examined by the spectator. The most convincing tricks are done if you use the spectator's very own deck. Whenever you can, borrow a deck.

There are many good effects that work by themselves. If presented properly, they will look like impossible miracles rather than self-working tricks. This one takes no practice.

Before you begin, secretly steal seven cards and hide them in your right-hand coat pocket. The backs of the cards should be toward your body.

Hand the deck to someone to shuffle.

"Think of any number between one and fifteen, then go through the cards and remember the card that is in that position. For example, if you think of number seven, look at the seventh card and remember it. Let someone else peek at your card if you like."

Having someone else peek at the card is insurance in case the first person forgets the name of the card. Wait until this is done, then take the deck back and set the cards on your palm.

"While I am holding the deck, your card is in the palm of my hand."

Put the deck into your right coat pocket. Make sure that it is facing the same way as the extra cards. The deck must go in front of the hidden cards. These cards will end up being the top cards of the deck when it comes out of your pocket.

> *"Now, do you know where your card is? It's in my pocket. Without touching the cards I shall attempt to move your card."*

Tap the outside of your pocket a few times.

> *"Where is your card now? In my pocket? Would you believe it's in Chicago?*

Bring the deck out of your pocket (with the added seven cards) and hand it to the spectator.

> *"What was the number you chose before?"*

We'll assume the number was four.

> *"Four? Then your card should be in the fourth position. Please count down four cards, deal them onto the table. Look at the last card. Is that your card? Of course it isn't. It's in Chicago."*

Wait for the reaction and then continue.

> *"Please spell the name Chicago by dealing one card on the table for each letter you spell. Spell out loud please."*

When he or she comes to the letter "o," you add:

> *"What was the name of your card? There it is right at the end of Chicago. Turn it over."*

The last card dealt will be the selected card. The number of letters in the name of the city you use will determine the number of cards in your pocket. Ohio needs four cards, Denver six cards, and so on. Do not use a long name or the deck will look too strange.

Coincidence

Two spectators and a full deck of 52 cards are required. Remove all the jokers if there are any. Have the deck fully shuffled before you begin.

> *"You will each need half a deck, so if one of you nice people will be so kind as to deal the cards, one card to each person until the deck is divided, we can begin."*

One person could also count 26 cards, but the first way shows that the cards are not in any special order.

> *"If each of you will take one pile and shuffle it, we will be ready. Have you done this? Good. Please reach into the center of your packets and remove a single card. Remember this card and place it on top of your packs."*

Take a pile from one spectator and place it on top of the other one. Then cut the deck in half and complete the cut.

"Your cards are lost in the pack."

Suggest that each one take turns in cutting the deck and replacing the cut so that the cards are *"hopelessly lost."* Choose one spectator.

"Please take the deck and count down twenty-six cards, dealing them one at a time. We will then have two packets."

When this has been done, allow the other person to select any one of the two piles by turning it face up.

"Please pick up your piles, one face up and one face down. You will each deal your cards onto the table, one card at a time. One person deal them face up, the other face down. Do this together. As you are dealing, keep an eye on the face-up pile. As soon as either one of you sees your card on that pile, call "stop" and you will both stop dealing. Go!"

When either of the two spectators sees his or her card, you then turn up the last card dealt on the face-down pile. It will prove to be the other's selected card.

"A perfect coincidence, you have both found your cards at the same time."

The Force

Most people have no idea that a magician can make them select a specific card. Let's keep it that way and cherish the secret known as "forcing." There are many ways to force a card but, as promised, we will not confuse you with sleight-of-hand methods at this time. A working knowledge of math gives us a simple force.

Let us say that you wish to force the ace of spades. Place this card in the ninth position from the top of the deck. Here is how to make your spectator select the ace.

"Think of any number between ten and twenty, please. Deal down that many cards while my back is turned. One card at a time, please. Have you done that?"

Wait a few moments for the spectator to deal.

"Just to make this a more random selection, I'd like you to add the digits of your number. If you counted twelve cards, numbers one and two in twelve gives you a total of three. Eighteen cards give you a one and an eight, which is nine. In this way you come up with a new number strictly by chance. Have you got that new number? Good. Now pick up the cards you just dealt on the table. Deal down as many cards as the new number you just chose. Three, four, five cards—whatever the total was. Look at the very next card. Remember it."

He or she will be looking at the ace of spades. Try this with various numbers between ten and twenty and see that it will always work.

To vary the trick you might put the ace in the tenth position, in which case your last instructions would be,

"Look at the last card you dealt" rather than the *"very next card."*

You are now in a position to create any astounding revelation you like.

Phantom Photo

This amazing revelation involves a force and a production. You will need a small picture frame, large enough to hold a playing card. Find an inexpensive frame that has three parts. The frame, a sheet of glass, and a cardboard back with an easel on it are the parts you need. (Fig. 95.) You will also need a handkerchief, a small bit of two-sided cellophane or masking tape, and a duplicate of the card you are going to force. Let us assume it's the two of clubs.

Back the two of clubs with a small bit of tape in the center of the card. Lay the card face down on the table, sticky side up. Place it somewhere behind another object so that it isn't obvious. The fully assembled frame is standing up with the empty area facing the audience. The handkerchief is in your pocket, and your deck is in readiness for the force of the two of clubs.

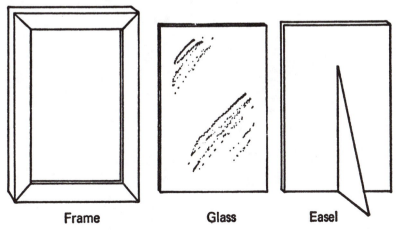

Frame   Glass   Easel

Fig. 95

Hand the deck to someone in the audience to *"hold for a few moments."*

"I'd like to show you something very interesting involving a combination of magic and photography. But first I'll need a frame for my picture."

Pick up the frame and show it around. Now remove the back and display it front and back. Casually set it on the table so that it is directly on top of the duplicate card. The tape will adhere to the front flat part of the easel piece (Fig. 96.) Now remove the glass and show it—*"solid, see-through glass."* The other hand holds up the frame for all to see.

Replace the glass sheet in the frame. Now casually lift the easel part so that the duplicate card is facing your body. The back easel faces the audience. The frame and glass are in toward your body as you replace the back easel in its frame. You will see the card showing in the frame, but the audience will not. Stand the frame on the table with its back to the audience and toss the hand-kerchief over it. A remark like *"Oops, wrong way!"* will give you an excuse to turn the frame around again so that the picture will face the audience when the handkerchief is removed later.

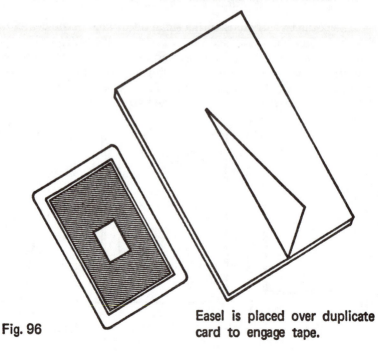

Fig. 96

Easel is placed over duplicate card to engage tape.

The dirty work has been done, and so far the audience will suspect nothing because you really haven't started the trick.

Have the spectator come up with the deck, remove it from its case, and force the two of clubs. *"Have you selected your card? Good, may we all see it? May I have it, please? It is the two of clubs."* Hold it up and bring it about five or six inches from the frame. Turn the card so that its face is toward the handkerchief.

"Instant photography by magic. Faster than Polaroid. One, two, three."

Whisk away the cloth and reveal the duplicate card in the frame.

For a more interesting revelation you could actually use a photograph of your force card rather than a duplicate.

KEY CARDS

The simplest and most direct way to locate a chosen card is with the "Key Card" method. Any known card placed next to an unknown card becomes your "Key." Find the known card and the selected card is easily identified.

Look at the bottom card of your deck and remember what it is. Now ask someone,

"Select a card, remember it, and put it on top of the deck."

Cut the deck and complete the cut. Your Key is now directly on top of his or her card. If you turn the deck face up in front of you and run through the cards, you can watch for your key. The card to its immediate right is the one he or she selected. The deck may even be given a single overhand shuffle, and the odds are that the two cards will not separate.

Using the Key Card as a locator, you can then proceed with a comic or dramatic revelation.

Card Stabbing

Use a small grocery bag and a sharp kitchen knife for this very startling revelation to find the selected card.

The knife and bag are on your table. Have a card selected in the manner just described so that you can use a Key Card location to find the card. The deck is cut and handed back to you.

Pick up the cards and run through the faces to find your Key.

"Your card is lost somewhere in this pack, and even if I look through them, there is no way to tell what it is."

While you are talking, you are really looking for the Key. Cut the deck when you find it so that the Key Card is now on the bottom again and the chosen card is back on top of the deck. Do not let the spectators see the cards.

Shake the bag open with your right hand and transfer it to your left, the hand that should now be holding the deck. The left thumb goes on the outside of the bag. The other hand and the deck are inside the bag. Slide the top card back a bit as you let all the other cards drop into the bag. (Fig. 97.) Your left hand will now be holding a single card against the inside wall of the bag.

Shake the bag up and down as you pick up the knife with the other hand.

"I have no idea where your card is now, but I'd like to take a stab at it anyway."

Push the knife from the outside of the bag through the center of the selected card and right on through the other side of the paper bag.

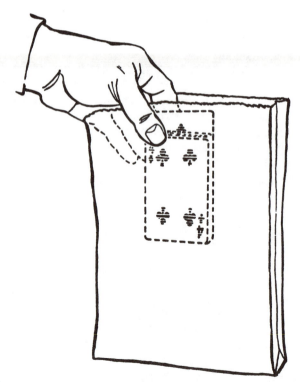

Fig. 97

With a downward motion pull the knife to the center of the bag, then straight out in front of you so that it tears through the paper. The cards may drop to the floor, but with a flourish and a look of triumph you will hold the knife aloft. The selected card is impaled on the knife.

Be extremely careful when handling the knife to avoid cutting yourself or spectators sitting too close. If you are on a stage, make sure the cards that fall are pushed out of the way so that people cannot slip on them later.

Hieroglyphics

This time our known Key Card will help us with a force. The handling is subtle and bold but quite effective and a lot of fun if presented tongue-in-cheek fashion. The Key Card is now the one on top of the deck. Let us say it is the ace of diamonds for our example. You can shuffle the cards as long as you don't disturb the top card. Use two spectators for this one. Hand the deck to one of the spectators for a moment. This person will be called spectator #2.

"Have you ever heard of the Egyptian 'Book of the Dead'? This was a book made up of pictures or hieroglyphics which were considered to be magic charms for dead people to take with them into the next world. They are very interesting, and I have studied a good many of them. Let me show you a fun experiment using the pictures."

Write two predictions on two small pieces of paper. The first prediction will read "ace of diamonds." Under the words draw a simple symbol or two. The next prediction will have only a few symbols but no written words. Fold the papers and hand the first one to spectator #1, the second one to the person holding the deck.

"Put the papers in your pocket—we'll use them later. Will you please think of a small number, then deal that many cards onto the table. Look at the last card you dealt and remember it."

Turn your back for a moment to allow this to be done in private.

"Put all the cards back on top. Hand the deck to your friend. But first whisper the number you chose."

Indicate spectator #1.

"Will you please deal that many cards onto the table one at a time. Look at the last card you dealt and place the deck on top of the pile on the table."

Fig. 98

By dealing the cards a second time, he or she is reversing the order to place the cards back to the original position, thereby forcing the ace of diamonds. The bottom card of the deck is now the card spectator #2 selected. Pick up the deck, get a secret look at the bottom card, and cut the cards to lose it. Let us assume it was the king of clubs. Turn to the second person.

"Please read the slip of paper I gave you earlier."

He will read the "ace of clubs."

"Do you see the hieroglyphic? That says ace of clubs. And what does yours say?"

Turn to the other spectator. He or she will have only a hieroglyphic. (Fig. 98.)

"Did I forget the translation? I'm sorry. Let me see it. Oh yes, see . . . it says right here, the king of clubs. Darn clever, those early Egyptians, weren't they?"

Short Corner Key

A valuable tool for the magician to use is a permanent key card. Of course, this cannot be used with a borrowed deck, but only with your own deck. Decide on the card you will always use as your key. I use the four of clubs because it has high visibility on a stage.

Use a small nail clipper to make your gimmicked card. The card should be face down on the table. Clip a very tiny tip off the upper left-hand corner of the card. Do the same with the opposite diagonal lower right corner. You must now trim the corner to round it so that it looks like the rest of the cards in the deck. Do this with a small sharp scissors.

Place the gimmicked card in the center of your deck. Hold the cards in the left hand, fingers on one side and thumb along the top of the other side, as in Fig. 99. Riffle the corners in a downward direction with your thumb. You will feel a small stop point. You may even hear a tiny click. The deck breaks easily at that point and, if you cut it, the short card may be brought to the

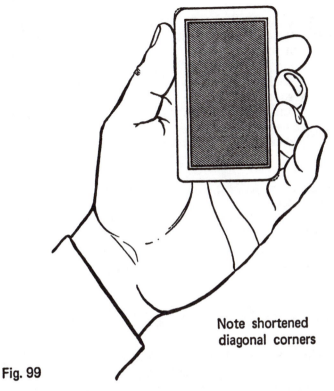

Note shortened
diagonal corners

Fig. 99

bottom of the deck. The gimmick you have just made is called a "corner short" and has many uses.

There is no longer any need for looking at the bottom card of the deck to glimpse a Key Card. Your thumb merely riffles, and you cut the deck so that your known key is on the bottom.

As a locator you need not look through the faces of the cards anymore. You can locate the selected card with a single riffle and cut to bring it to the top of the deck.

If you make your "short" card when the deck is new, the color of the corner will be same as the rest of the deck, so it is virtually undetectable to the eye.

Quick Reversal

Have the selected card placed on top of the deck, cut the deck, and ask that the spectator shuffle it. Indicate an overhand shuffle by moving your hands up and down, pantomiming this type of mix. As soon as he or she starts the shuffle, extend your hand. This will give time for only a short shuffle, since the spectator knows you want the cards back. A shuffle of this sort should not divide the key and selected cards.

Take the deck behind your back, riffle the edge, and locate the gimmicked short card. Cut the deck so that the selected card is now on top. Turn it upside-down and place it in the center of the pack. Bring the pack out front.

"Your card was the six of spades, is that right?"

You are probably wrong. In case you really guess it, call it a miracle.

"No? Then it must be king of hearts, right?"

You are wrong again.

"Did you put it back? Right side up? Let's check. What card was it?"

As he or she names the card, you spread the face-down cards across the table. The selected card will appear face up in the spread.

A Good Ear for Clubs

The gimmicked short-corner key is used again for this fun effect. Have the card selected and returned to the top, then cover it with the key when you cut the deck.

"Was your card a heart, diamond, club, or spade?"

Let us say a club was selected.

"Club. That's great—I have a good ear for clubs."

Bring the deck up to your ear and riffle the corners. As soon as you hear the click, cut the deck at that point.

"That's it. I hear a club. What was the name of the card?"

Turn the card face up to show that you have found it.

Out of the Pocket

You can use most any kind of revelation when you have the location made by any method. We'll assume you used the corner short and brought the selected card to the top of your deck. Put the entire deck in your pocket.

"Please give me any small number between one and twenty."

Let us say the number was nine. Start taking cards out of your pocket one at a time, taking them from the bottom of the deck.

When you come to the ninth card, take that one from the top and reveal it to be the selected card.

You can make up many more revelations. Drop the deck into a paper bag as you did with the stabbing trick. Instead of stabbing the selected card, you could pretend you found it by sense of touch from among the mixed cards.

EIGHT KINGS

The instantaneous location of selected cards can be accomplished with the use of a stacked or set-up deck. In *Magic with Cards* we talked about the Si Stebbins arrangement of cards that was very practical for mental effects. The arrangement was such that by looking at the bottom card of the deck you could instantly name the top card.

The sequence of cards had a specific pattern where each card had the value of three more than the preceding card. If a Si Stebbins deck were spread face up across a table, an astute mathematician might recognize the 3-6-9 pattern.

The Eight Kings setup has no logical sequence. The deck is arranged and memorized with the help of a poem.

> Eight Kings threatened to save,
> Ninety-five ladies for one sick knave.

Broken down carefully, the code names all thirteen cards.

Eight—King—Three—Ten (threatened) Two—Seven(save)
Nine—Five—Queen (ladies)—Four—Ace (one)—Six (sick)—
Jack (knave)

Study it again to see how the words represent the cards. With a minimum of time the poem can be learned so that you can call off the cards in order. Practice this once or twice.

To determine the suits, the cards again must be arranged in a known sequence. One easy way to set them up is by remembering the word CHaSeD. The words in capital letters indicate the suits: C—Clubs; H—Hearts; S—Spades; D—Diamonds.

Here is how a thirteen-card series would read in the eight-kings setup.

8C—KH—3S—10D—2C—7H—9S—5D—QC—4H—AS—3D—JC

After the Jack, the next eight begins the series again. (8H—KS—3D . . . etc.)

The cards may be spread across a table, and no one will ever see a logical numerical sequence. Set up a deck in the Eight-Kings series.

Cut the cards as many times as you like. Cutting the cards does not destroy the sequence. Now look at the bottom card. Let's assume it is the six of hearts (sick). The next card in sequence must be the Jack (knave). Since spades always follow hearts, the top card will be the Jack of spades. Practice cutting the deck and reading the top cards until you have mastered it. It should become second nature to you.

Have a card selected from the center of your deck. Cut the deck at that point. All the cards that were above the selected card are cut to the bottom. A quick look at the bottom card will tell you the name of the selected card.

You can have three or four cards removed in one block and name all of them almost by reciting the poem.

X-ray Eyes

Your deck is set with an Eight-Kings setup. As you speak, you casually cut the cards a few times. Now turn the deck face up on the table. Ask a spectator to cut the face-up pack once more, replacing the cut.

"Do you think it would be possible for anyone to see clear through a deck this thick? Probably not. But I'm going to try. Please cut about a third of the cards to a pile at the right. Cut another pile and place it in the center. Let me look right through the cards."

The bottom card showing at the right will tell you the name of the card under the extreme left-hand pile. It will be the next card in the series. The bottom card of the left-hand pile will tell you the name of the card buried under the middle pile. The top face card of the middle pile tells you the name of the right-hand hidden bottom card. With all the cards face up, start from left to right, pretending to look clear through the middle of each card. As you name each of the cards under the face-up piles, slide them out and set them aside face up on the table.

Triple Reversal

This is a blockbuster effect that can be performed as the last trick

of the evening. It is very strong and should not be followed by
another card trick.

You will need two decks of contrasting colors, both arranged
in the Eight-Kings setup. We'll assume you are using red and blue
decks. Cut both decks so that their face cards will not be same. Put
them into their own boxes and leave them on the table ready for
the performance.

Call a spectator on the stage. Pick up the cards, one deck in
each hand.

*"Please select one of these two decks, red or blue. Whichever
deck you choose you will use."*

It makes no difference which pack he takes.

*"Remove the deck from the case and look through the cards
to make sure they are not arranged in any way. Now please
cut the pack and set the cards face down on your palm."*

Do not allow him too much time to look through the cards. Once
you said they were not arranged, he would be foolish to think
otherwise. (That's what he would think.)

*"Take the deck behind your back, please, and cut the cards
once more. Replace the cut. You may cut them again if you
like."*

Wait until he is ready.

*"Ready? Okay. Now please take the top three cards and one
at a time insert them upside down into the middle of the pack.
Are they lost? Good. May I have the cards, please?"*

Take the cards from him and in the act of setting them on the
table get a look at the bottom card. Let's assume it is the eight of
diamonds.

"I will leave the cards here and do not wish to handle them."

Pick up the other deck and remove the cards from their case.
Step over to the spectator and show him the faces of the cards,
running through them quickly. You are looking for the eight of
diamonds as you do this.

*"You could have selected this pack which is not arranged in
any way, is that so, sir?"*

He will usually agree.

When you find the eight, cut it to the bottom of your pack.
Bring the deck behind your back.

*"Neither you nor I have any idea what cards were reversed in
your deck. I will do the same as you. I will take the deck behind my back and will take three cards, one at a time. I will
insert them reversed into the middle of the deck."*

Do this as you say it. It is okay if the audience sees you taking the top cards and putting them into the center of the deck. Place your deck on the table next to his.

"*You took the red cards, I took the blue. I will not touch the decks again. Please spread the cards and describe what you see. The three face-up cards in your pack are identical to the ones in my pack. Is this a coincidence, sir? It is not! It is magic!*"

HANDLING YOUR DECK

When doing card tricks, you are supposed to be the master of your trade. Therefore, I suggest you take the time to work with a deck of cards so that you look good.

Learn how to shuffle properly. Learn how to cut the cards neatly and deftly. Spread the deck properly so that your spectator can get a card out easily.

This section is devoted to showing you the proper way to handle your cards. There are no tricks described, but each point is very valuable.

The first thing I suggest that you work with is the Key Cut.

Key Cut

Hold the deck in your left hand, thumb on one side and four fingers on the other. Your left palm is cupped slightly. (Fig. 100.)

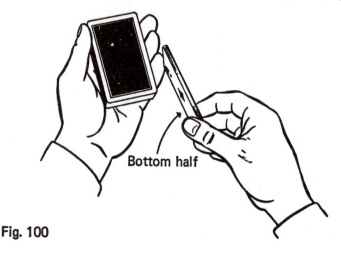

Bottom half

Fig. 100

The right hand must come over the top of the cards. You will take the pack from the left hand with the thumb and middle fingers of the right hand. But only take the bottom half away. The cards in the left hand drop into the left palm, and the right hand deposits its half on top of them. The deck is cut.

Let's assume you have a Key Card on the bottom of the deck. A card has been selected. You start the Key Cut, pulling the bottom section away. Have the card replaced on top of the remaining cards in the left hand. Cover it with the cards in the right, and your Key is on top of the selected card, which is now somewhere in the middle of the pack rather than on top.

Overhand Shuffle

Hold the deck in your left hand as in Fig. 101. The cards are facing the left thumb, with the deck lying on its side. The right hand cuts off the bottom half and brings it back on top of the left hand. The left thumb will pull off a small bunch of cards and the right hand moves away. Repeat the same action with the right hand coming over the left until all the cards have been shuffled

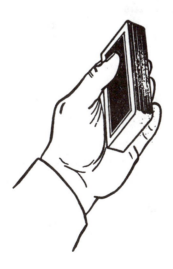

Fig. 101

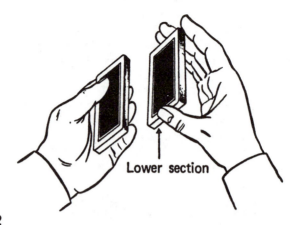

Lower section

Fig. 102

into the left hand. Then do it all over again. It really looks like a series of small cuts. (Fig. 102.)

If you want to leave the key card on the bottom of the deck, your right hand can cut off the top half of the deck and shuffle those back without disturbing the bottom stack.

Here is how to keep the top card in place. Hold the deck in the right hand and pull off only the top card with the left thumb. Then continue to shuffle the right cards into the left hand. This brings the top card to the bottom of the deck. Now shuffle again, this time making sure that the very last bottom card from the right hand stack will fall last. You have brought the bottom card back to the top again.

Spreading the Cards

Hold the deck in the left hand, face down, as though you were going to deal. Begin by pushing the cards from left to right with your left thumb. The right hand will receive the cards palm up. The right thumb holds onto the top card, while the right fingers pull the cards into the right hand. The left will feed them, as the right receives them. This offers an open spread for the spectator to have a good choice of cards. (Fig. 103.)

Fig.103

Switching a Deck

This is required only when you have to introduce a set-up deck, such as the Eight-Kings deck. Have the set-up deck in your left coat pocket, lying across the pocket. Use a regular deck that matches the stacked deck. After you have done a few tricks, put the cards back in their case and set the deck in the same left coat pocket. This time, stand the deck up in the pocket. As a second thought remove the deck (the stacked one) and toss it on the table. Wait a few moments before picking it up again. It will appear that you are still using the same cards.

PROPS

There be divers juggling boxes with false bottoms, wherein manie false feates are wrought.

Reginald Scot, DISCOVERIE OF WITCHCRAFT, 1584
Book XIII, Chapter XXXI

A FEW WORDS ABOUT PROPS

A magician is expected to be a magician wherever he goes. People expect that he can make things disappear or appear at his will at any time of the day or night. It would be quite impractical for you to carry your bag of tricks around with you everywhere. That is why you should learn to deal with common unprepared items.

As you can tell from the title of my last book, I am a firm believer in performing *Magic with Everyday Objects.* The sleight-of hand vanishes can be done anywhere with borrowed coins or other small objects. When asked to perform magic on the spur of the moment, you can do many impromptu miracles. Produce a quarter, then make it vanish and reappear. With a few paper cups and bits of a napkin you are ready for the Cups and Balls. The Gypsy method of reading thoughts is always available to you. Borrow a deck of cards. Always be ready to create magic on short notice. Once your friends know you are interested in the art, they will constantly expect miracles and the impossible. Make it possible.

To keep interest in your magic, you must use things that are within the common experience of your spectators. The magic should not look as if it relies on props. Things used should be familiar to your audience. They should be natural-looking objects, and the reasons you offer for doing what you are doing should be simple and logical. Your patter should be in a simple, uncomplicated language that is natural to you.

Any stage prop you use must look like something they have seen before. A paper bag is a normal item since everyone is familiar with it. A similar container or bag made of tinsel and sequins will surely arouse suspicion. It is too uncommon. The natural-looking prop must take priority over the ornate one.

If you must use something unusual in size or shape, there should be a reason for its being. A painted mirror box can be described as an oriental tea chest. It will be acceptable because it has a logical use. An interesting story will take suspicion away from a prop like a Tube of Plenty. You can call it an antique belonging to a famous person in history; or perhaps explain that it comes from a faraway place. It is odd, but people believe that objects coming from foreign countries should look unusual. Since their experiences are limited, they will accept that people elsewhere use objects that are different from ours.

This book describes props that can, for the most part, be made of common, everyday objects. They must not look like props and certainly should not distract from the effectiveness of the illusion.

BORROWING

The borrowed item is always above suspicion. If you can, it is always advisable to borrow the items you use in your magic. Always ask nicely and in a gentle manner, never demanding. At first, people may be reluctant to offer you their valuable items, but once they know it is for fun and their entertainment, they will cooperate. Always be prepared with your own prop, just in case you do run into cautious spectators.

I perform a trick where I borrow, then burn and restore a handkerchief. I find that people are often embarrassed to lend you a very personal item since it may be soiled or torn, etc. I carry a few spares and will hand one to a person sitting nearby before the show. I'll ask him to lend it to me in case I need it. If I burned my own handkerchief, it would not be as funny.

Card tricks are most effective when you borrow the deck. Borrowing money will assure that at least the lender will give you his undivided attention. The rest of the audience loves to see what will happen to the person's money.

Be sure that you always return the items you borrow in good shape and with plenty of graciousness and thanks. You'll want these people to remember that you are a nice guy and they'll ask you to entertain them again some day.

GIMMICKS

The gimmick is the secret, unseen helper that is used by the magician. The quiet pull that takes a handkerchief away is a gimmick. The Mirror Box is called a gimmicked box because it was prepared to help you hide the production items. The mirror itself is called a feke (pronounced just like *fake*) because while it is a gimmick, it is not hidden but seen by the spectator. It is seen but never suspected to be anything else but the bottom or rear of the box. The glass without the bottom is a feke. It is seen by the audience but never suspected to be anything other than a normal glass.

There are many things that can be feked or gimmicked, as you will see as you delve deeper into this fascinating art. The short corner card is a feke; the glued dollar bill and five is a feke bill; the knife with two colors is a feke knife; and so on.

It is very important that the spectators do not know that normal objects can be feked. People will never suspect money to be prepared in any way. People have heard that cards may be marked, but never shorted. It is vital to your success that you honor the secrets of magic. The gimmicks are most secret of all.

ENTERTAIN

13

Just let me entertain you and we'll have a real good time, yes sir,—"

"Let Me Entertain you," GYPSY, by Jule Styne and Stephen Sondheim.

ROUTINING + PATTER + PRESENTATION = ENTERTAINMENT

The secret formula described above is your door to the success of your performances. It applies to magic and comedy as well as any other forms of performing art. The purpose of mastering your skills and demonstrating them should be expressed in a single word—entertainment.

Before every show I find myself singing the words of a popular song from the show *Gypsy. "Let me entertain you, let me make you smile."* And onstage I find myself following the words: *"Let me do a few tricks, some old and then some new tricks. I'm very versatile."*

I do not recommend you talking to yourself, but I do strongly state my motto: *"Entertainment first, magic second."* If you ask me what I do for a living, I will answer, *"I'm a entertainer."* My specialty is magic. Keep this in mind and you will not let the tricks and the secrets of magic detract from the purpose of performing it.

Entertaining people is one of the greatest accomplishments you will realize in your life. To be able to make people happy, keep their interest, stimulate their thinking, and brighten their lives is a wonderful talent to achieve. Entertainment is not only making people laugh, it also involves giving them a sense of pleasure, relaxation, or general good feeling toward you and your performance.

How do we do it? Glad you asked.

ROUTINING

Your routine is your method of presenting your material in a specific sequence that you have prepared in advance. The tricks and bits are laid out in a special order that you will follow each time you perform. The sequence you select should be interesting from beginning to end. That sequence becomes your act.

Your act will have three parts—an opening, middle, and a closing. Your object is to get your audience interested in what you are doing as soon as possible. You must do this in your opening. The tricks that follow the opening, in the body of your act, must be chosen to sustain that interest and keep their attention. The final, closing effect should be the best or most amazing thing you do. This will leave your audience wanting more of the same. Routine your act to have a strong opening, a good flowing middle section, and a very powerful closing.

Before you can even consider your routine, you should make sure that you know every trick and move by heart. Every effect must be properly rehearsed so that you could almost do it in your sleep. Every detail should be noted and every move choreographed so that you know when to walk to your table, when to turn, when to pick up an object, etc. This will assure that your stage appearance will not look haphazard. You must be in command of your act at all times.

Select your material carefully so that you do not duplicate effects of the same kind. You want a variety in the props you use and the kinds of tricks you perform. Balance colorful effects and sleights with different types of magic. You would not cut and restore a rope and then follow it by tearing and restoring a napkin. The two are basically the same to the audience. Pace your effects, and make sure you sprinkle your vanishes and productions in with the transformations and restorations.

Select a short, flashy trick that you can do fairly quickly for your opening effect. You want to get your audience's attention immediately with a snappy effect. Look for tricks with color that might be accompanied by bright music to stimulate a feeling of excitement and anticipation of things to come.

Select your strongest effect for the closing number. Now go back to the beginning of the act. You might make a list of the tricks you do and put them on 3 x 5 inch cards. Spread the cards out on a table in front of you and rearrange them into a flowing sequence. Avoid selecting too many tricks. A long act can lose your audience's attention span.

Check your tricks for color, comedy, and the kinds of effects that will follow one another. Use a bit of logic. Perhaps the last thing you produce from your production box can be the focal object of the next trick. Do not have too many audience-participation effects. Do most of the magic yourself—after all, it *is* your act. Keep the effects relatively short and without a lot of time lost in counting or detailed instructions. Something must be happening on stage at all times. Tricks that run too long slow down the act and are hard to follow.

Now that you have what you think is a good routine, rehearse the entire act and time it. If you will be doing an act where you are the only performer, a 45-minute routine is usually enough. If the act is geared for variety shows where you will be working with other performers, 15 to 18 minutes is sufficient.

Always be flexible and ready for change after you have tested the act a few times. Test different sequences of the same tricks until you come up with a routine you think is good. You may weed out the weaker effects and add a few new ones. Your audience will tell you which tricks they like best. Watch the applause, or tape your show and listen to the reactions. Whatever act you finally decide upon must be comfortable for you to do. You must work with the routine until you look natural doing it. That is your act.

PATTER

Patter is the spoken word used by the performer. It is what he or she is saying as the trick is performed. Patter can be used to provide misdirection, offer instructions, create laughter, or keep the audience's attention. If you use patter, there are some rules that you can follow to make sure you keep the audience with you.

Find the proper delivery, the best way for you to speak. Fast talkers may lose audiences because they do not allow people enough time to digest what they have heard. Slow talkers can put audiences to sleep. A high-pitched speaker sounds nervous and might make an audience ill at ease. A low pitch can irritate the listener. It is therefore up to you to find a happy medium by testing your own vocal qualities. Your quality should be pleasing to hear. The voice must not distract from your actions unless you want it to do so. Keep a constant volume, loud enough to be heard but not loud enough to disturb someone's eardrums. Do not adopt a monotone, but try to vary your pitch with highs and lows that emphasize your words. Keep the speed within limits so that your audience won't be out of breath as you speak. Speak distinctly, making sure that every word is understood and not garbled.

Make sure you are articulate and use your language correctly. Improper grammar can destroy your image, so learn to speak correctly and to avoid slang. Try not to use words that are too fancy for your average audience. You don't want to sound like a snob or a highbrow. You want to make yourself understood at all times.

Do not memorize your material word for word. Learn to find the key phrases that are important to your magic. Try not to recite your lines, but rather merely talk them. Do not learn the patter in this book exactly as written. Use the ideas until you can develop your own way of presenting the tricks. Make up your own words and be yourself.

Never be afraid to adlib. Say whatever you think is right for the situation as long as it is in good taste and does not insult anyone. Have a few quips ready for odd situations that might occur. You can collect some of the adlibs used by other performers until you can come up with your own.

Patter does not have to be funny. Remember that you are a magician, not a comedian. Very few magicians can deliver gags without losing the integrity of the magic. But do use humor as often as possible, and keep your performance light. You can add comedy with the situations you present rather than stock comedy lines. If you kid yourself, you can gain laughter and earn some respect at the same time. Exaggeration makes for good comedy. Call something large that is small. Mild failure on your part also creates laughs. Pretend that the trick didn't work and then make it work at last. Repetition offers comedy. You can repeat some magic words that never work. But never overdo the comedy, as it could ruin the picture of the magician you are trying to paint.

No patter will be effective unless you are heard. If your

audience cannot hear you, nothing will help. Whenever possible, use a microphone so you won't have to shout. The microphone should be about six inches from your mouth. Try not to swallow it. If you do a lot of walking around during your performance, you might use a neck mike (lavalier). If you use this, be sure you learn how to handle the trailing wire that will follow you and most certainly get in your way. I use a small clip on my belt. I can hook the wire off to my side so that it trails behind me.

Many acts do not use patter at all. If you intend to do a "silent" act, every effect must "speak" for itself. You must communicate with the audience by the use of your facial expressions and hand gestures. These should be slightly exaggerated. Every move should be very obvious, detailed, and visible to all parts of your audience. Good music should be behind you to effect the transition from trick to trick and to relax the audience as they watch your manipulations.

PRESENTATION

The art of performing is involved with expressing yourself in front of an audience in order to please them. Most people are interested in other people. The tricks you do can be done by many other magicians. It is, therefore, not only the tricks that concern your audience, they want to meet you. While selling entertainment, you must also sell yourself.

A trick is interesting to the audience because you are interesting. They want to see what you are doing with that trick. You are different from the average spectator. You can accomplish things that other people cannot. Their everyday existence may be dull or boring. Your work is exciting to them. Prove it. Be yourself, and make yourself the unusual individual they expect you to be.

Your audience will begin to evaluate you from the moment you walk onto the stage, first as a person and then as the magician. Your walk must be authoritative, your appearance and dress should be impressive, well tailored and prosperous. Your grooming must be neat—hair combed, hands clean, makeup perfect. Your suit or costume must be clean and pressed. This will be the first picture you present to your audience. If they are pleased with what they see, they will be in a frame of mind to be pleased with your act.

When you start to speak, don't disappoint them. Be articulate handling these people. Most people will be reluctant to volunteer to come onto the stage for fear that they will not look their best or that they may be intimidated. Put them at ease. Look for a person who is enjoying the show. He or she will be wearing a nice smile. Approach the situation with nice words.

"There's a pretty lady who might be able to assist me. I'd be honored to have you help."

or

"How about that handsome gentleman? Would you like to join the fun and give me a hand?"

Children must be handled differently. If there are more than a few, you must never ask directly. If you ask for an assistant to come onstage, you are mobbed with anxious youngsters before you can finish your sentence. If you want a child to assist, try this.

"Raise your hand if you'd like to assist me. I need a quiet boy or girl."

Once your volunteer is on the stage, be very polite. Request every action with a *"please"* up front and a *"thank you"* afterward. A little special attention gives your volunteer a comfortable feeling. The audience will also be at ease, and this will facilitate your getting another volunteer when you need one.

So now you have a good routine, patter, and an act. The music begins, the emcee announces your name, and off you go. Your heart flutters, you start to perspire, the pulse rate goes up, and there is a great feeling of excitement people call "stagefright." Stagefright is not fright at all, it is a normal reaction to the situation. It is an ailment that your body creates to tell you that all your body functions are in good order. The athlete feels it before a game, the pilot gets it before a takeoff, and you will have it before a show. It is an ailment you can cure.

The more frequently you perform, the easier it becomes. You know your act perfectly. Your costumes and props are set. You have confidence in what you are doing. Your stagefright disappears.

Presentation involves all the aspects of showmanship. It is a blend of all the knowledge you accumulate with performing experience. It involves timing, movement, comedy, laughter, color, music, personality, surprise, authority, stage presence, appearance, and charm. Look at these words again and learn how to master their meaning:

Routine + Patter + Presentation = Entertainment

so that they can understand everything you say and every instruction you give. Move about the stage with the authority that proves you belong there. You are polite and gracious. You are pleasant and graceful. Smile when you need to and laugh at yourself, never taking on an air of superiority. You are different from your audience, but not better than they are. If they like you, they will like your act. Even if something should go wrong, they will forgive you and root for you. They want to be on your side to help you entertain them.

You will encounter different kinds of audiences. Certain groups will react differently from other groups. For example, if you perform for one or two people, your presentation should be informal and relaxed. You won't have to project your voice and image, but will speak in normal tones as though you were conversing with them. A larger group will be noisier and perhaps mixed with people of different ages. To appeal to everyone in that group you must keep your magic routine interesting and select material that is universally appealing. Long-winded effects might bore some, and you don't want to risk losing them. A family audience likes color, music, and good, clean audience participation. A teen audience will be a critical group interested in impressing their peers with their knowledge. For this group you can keep away from puzzle-type tricks and present short, quick, funny effects that do not challenge their minds.

Children are very difficult to fool with misdirection since they are not sophisticated enough to take your hints. If you say a coin is in your hand, they will reply *"Oh, yeah? Let's see!"* This kind of audience wants fun. Use sucker effects, laugh-provoking situations, and audience participation involving colorful prop magic. Balloons and colorful silks will impress them more than manipulative skills.

The club-date audience needs different handling. A club, lodge, banquet, or social group hiring you as a featured entertainer for the evening will sit for longer effects. Here you can use more serious mindreading tricks or blockbuster and brain-teaser magic.

Knowing your audience will help you present the kind of magic they find interesting. No matter which audience you encounter, remember that no trick should be more important to you than the impression it makes on your audience.

People like to be fooled but not made to be fools. Keep in mind that you must never underestimate the intelligence of your audience. The success or failure of many of your efforts will be in the hands of the volunteer from the audience.

FINAL WORDS

Performing is the most exciting and exhilarating experience a person can achieve. It cannot be described in any book. To feel it, you must try it. Entertaining others is not just an ego trip. It is a privilege. Enjoy it!

BIBLIOGRAPHY

Barnett, Joseph. *Barnett on Sleights*. New York: Nonex Press, 1955.

Bobo, J. B. *Modern Coin Magic*. Minneapolis: C. W. Jones, 1952.

Christopher, Milbourne. *Houdini: The Untold Story*. New York: Crowell Publ., 1969

Christopher, Milbourne. *The Illustrated History of Magic*. New York: Thomas Y. Crowell, 1973.

Fitzkee, Dariel. *Magic by Misdirection*. Oakland: Magic Limited, 1975.

Garcia, Frank, and George Schindler. *Amedeo's Continental Magic*. New York: Million Dollar Productions, 1974.

Garcia, Frank, and George Schindler. *Magic with Cards*. New York: David McKay, 1975.

Hay, Henry. *Cyclopedia of Magic*. New York: David McKay, 1949.

Rydell, Wendy, and George Gilbert. *The Great Book of Magic*. New York: Harry N. Abrams, 1976.

Schindler, George. *Beginner's Curriculum*. New York: School for Magicians, Inc., 1973.

Schindler, George. *Magic with Everyday Objects*. New York: Stein & Day, 1976.

Scot, Reginald. *The Discoverie of Witchcraft*. 1584. New York: Dover Books, 1972 (reprint of 1886 edition).

Severn, Bill. *Bill Severn's Big Book of Magic*. New York: David McKay, 1973.

INDEX